Exploring the Basic Income Guarantee

Series Editor
Karl Widerquist, Georgetown University in Qatar, Doha, Qatar

Basic income is one of the most innovative, powerful, straightforward, and controversial proposals for addressing poverty and growing inequalities. A Basic Income Guarantee (BIG) is designed to be an unconditional, government-insured guarantee that all citizens will have enough income to meet their basic needs. The concept of basic, or guaranteed, income is a form of social provision and this series examines the arguments for and against it from an interdisciplinary perspective with special focus on the economic and social factors. By systematically connecting abstract philosophical debates over competing principles of BIG to the empirical analysis of concrete policy proposals, this series contributes to the fields of economics, politics, social policy, and philosophy and establishes a theoretical framework for interdisciplinary research. It will bring together international and national scholars and activists to provide a comparative look at the main efforts to date to pass unconditional BIG legislation across regions of the globe and will identify commonalities and differences across countries drawing lessons for advancing social policies in general and BIG policies in particular.

Karl Widerquist

The Problem of Property

Taking the Freedom of Nonowners Seriously

palgrave
macmillan

Karl Widerquist
Georgetown University in Qatar
Doha, Qatar

ISSN 2662-3803 ISSN 2662-3811 (electronic)
Exploring the Basic Income Guarantee
ISBN 978-3-031-21947-4 ISBN 978-3-031-21948-1 (eBook)
https://doi.org/10.1007/978-3-031-21948-1

This Palgrave Macmillan imprint is published by the registered company Springer Nature Switzerland AG
The registered company address is: Gewerbestrasse 11, 6330 Cham, Switzerland

Acknowledgments

This book is based on one part of the thesis[1] I wrote at Oxford between 2003 and 2006. The acknowledgments for that thesis were published in my 2013 book.[2] I began rewriting it for publication in 2022 and haven't shown the recent drafts to anyone. So, there are only a few new acknowledgments to mention.

First is my wife, Elizabeth Smith Widerquist, who tolerates my work, understands what I'm going through, and is loving in a way that makes me strong. My father, mother, siblings, my siblings' children, and my friends have given me support in many ways that have indirectly contributed to this project.

Part of the reason I decided to publish this book now came from an anonymous Twitter follower who found my thesis (which I had not promoted) and alerted me to the value of the chapters that were still unpublished.

Otto Lehto also helped inspire me to publish this book by pressing me to explain my own property theory.

[1] Widerquist, Karl (2006). *Property and the Power to Say No: A Freedom-Based Argument for Basic Income.* Oxford University: Department of Politics and International Relations.

[2] Widerquist, Karl (2013). *Independence, Propertylessness, and Basic Income: A Theory of Freedom as the Power to Say No.* New York: Palgrave Macmillan.

Ian Almond gave me very valuable advice just as I was finishing these revisions, as did several of my colleagues at the Economic Ethics Network meeting in Greece in 2022. Carole Sargent has given me incredibly valuable advice about all aspects of writing and publishing since I started at Georgetown in 2009.

Meera Seth, the managing editor of Palgrave's series "Exploring the Basic Income Guarantee" and the rest of Palgrave's team involved with this project have been extremely helpful.

I received support this year from the Goertz Werner Chair and the Freiburg Institute for Basic Income Studies at Albert-Ludwigs-Universität Freiburg.

I wrote large portions of this book at coffee shops on at least three continents. Thanks to all the baristas, janitors, and other employees at all those places, not to mention the janitors and support staff at the Department of Politics at the University of Oxford, in Freiburg, and the various buildings I've worked in.

I would like to thank Georgetown University-Qatar, its parent organizations Qatar Foundation, and the government of Qatar for my job and generous research support. Even more so, I would like to thank my colleagues and Georgetown-Qatar and the university's support staff. Most of all, I would like to thank the 100-plus migrant laborers who work *at* Georgetown but who don't officially work *for* Georgetown. Although most of them are essential workers without whom Georgetown-Qatar could not function, they are badly exploited, underpaid, overworked, separated from their families for years at a time, and not what you could call genuinely free laborers. Georgetown and Qatar Foundation tend to blame all mistreatment on human-resource companies that act as intermediaries, but the labors in our building provide services exclusively for us. Their mistreatment ends when we demand it. Here's the hope that Georgetown will make that demand and will be ready to close its operations in Qatar unless there is a major transformation in the treatment of labor on our campus. Here's also to the hope that pressure like that from individuals and international institutions will end the mistreatment of migrant laborers in both Qatar and in my home country, the United States of America.

—Karl Widerquist at Anis Café in Msheireb, Doha, Qatar on August 22, 2022.

Contents

CHAPTER 1

Introduction

As I went walking, a sign stopped me.
On the one side, it said "No Trespassing."
But on the other side, it didn't say nothing.
That side was made for you and me.
...
This land was made for you and me.
—Woody Guthrie, "This Land Is Your Land" as covered by Remember Alice?[1]

Any conception of a right—whether legal or natural—has to be reciprocal in the relevant ethic respect. A nonreciprocal "right" is merely a privilege. A right of self-ownership at least prima facie passes this test. It amounts to saying accept my ownership of my body as I respect your ownership of your body. The highly unequal ownership system that prevails in external assets (i.e., property in anything outside of our living bodies) prima facie fails this test in at least two ways. First, it gives one group control over resources essential to everyone's survival and therefore, forces the propertyless group to perform services for the

[1] Guthrie, Woody (1956). "This Land Is Your Land." Woody Guthrie Publications, Inc. & TRO Ludlow Music, Inc. (BMI), covered by Remember Alice? c. 1996.

K. Widerquist, *The Problem of Property*, Exploring the Basic Income Guarantee, https://doi.org/10.1007/978-3-031-21948-1_1

property-owning group to survive. Second, it amounts to saying, "You should respect my property for I would respect yours if you had any."[2]

My 2006 dissertation, *Property and the Power to Say No*,[3] addressed both of these problems with property from what I now call an "indepentarian" perspective. That thesis also represented my first detailed statement of what I now call "Justice as the Pursuit of Accord" (JPA). It addressed both of the above objections to the property rights system.

By 2013, I managed to expand the freedom section—the part addressing the first of the two objections mentioned above—into a full-length book, *Independence, Propertylessness, and Basic Income: A Theory of Freedom as the Power to Say No*.[4] I intended to later expand the parts addressing the second objection into a full-length book of its own. Nearly 10 years later, I had not yet made good on that intention, and only one chapter from that part of the book had been published as an article. Therefore, I decided to publish the property section of my thesis as this short book.

I did minimal updates and changes to the original manuscript. The biggest change is that Chapter 3, "Lockean Property Theory," is a summary (with minor changes) of the version of the thesis chapter that was published in *Public Reason* in 2010.[5]

I also made some small changes, including copyediting and a few updates to the terminology, such as, changing "he or she" to "they," and where appropriate, I now use "Universal Basic Income" (UBI) rather than "Basic Income," or "Unconditional Basic Income." As I copyedited the book, I could not resist updating some of the text to reflect how my writing style and thinking have developed in the last 15 years, but I tried to keep those changes to a minimum. I have made only minimal updates to the citations, and some of the citations will, therefore, be dated, but the arguments addressed here are still underexplored in the literature.

I submitted the dissertation on which this book is based before I settled on the terms "indepentarianism" and "justice as the pursuit of accord," but most of the elements that make up those concepts are in place here,

[2] Waldron J. (1988). *The Right to Private Property*. Oxford: Clarendon Press, 441.

[3] Widerquist, *Property and the Power*.

[4] Widerquist, *Independence*.

[5] Widerquist, Karl (2010). "Lockean Theories of Property: Justifications for Unilateral Appropriation." *Public Reason* 2 (3): 3–26.

one central example being the existence of dissenters (people who have reasonable objections to prevailing social arrangements, the duties they are asked to perform, or the rewards they are given in return). The presence of dissenters represents the failure of social contract theory or natural rights theory to create social arrangements that no reasonable person could object to or that all rational ethical people must accept. Most political theories have dealt with dissenters by wishing them away: each theorist assumes their contract or their conception of natural rights is the one that no ethical person could reasonably reject. I instead assume that nobody's theory will ever be that good—and that includes my theory and the theories of the dissenters themselves should they come to power.[6]

If I'm right, the problem of justice is not how to come up with an imaginary agreement or list of rights that we can tell ourselves no reasonable person could reject. We should doubt the value of any philosopher's imagined consensus of all supposedly reasonable people either to a social contract or to a set of natural rights, because both the theory and practice of politics inherently advantages insiders and disadvantages outsiders.

Also, if I'm right, the problem of justice is to obtain the literal agreement of as many people as possible while minimizing interference with and oppression of dissenters and of disadvantaged people (understood as people who might not know they have good reason to dissent).

JPA theory is "indepentarian" in the sense that it gives a high priority to the independence of each individual. Ideally, we would all live together in accord—under rules that we all *literally* agree on. If we cannot agree, the next best solution is to divide into separate communities, each of which can do things their way. Because we are effectively stuck together, the majority must get their way, but they have the responsibility to be aware that they are imposing their will on dissenters. Therefore, they take on a responsibility to respect individual independence as much as possible and to forever pursue literal, present agreement with everyone by minimizing the negative effects the social order imposes on dissenters and disadvantaged people. Justice is something we *pursue* but never fully capture.

[6] Widerquist, Karl (2019). "The Pursuit of Accord: Toward a Theory of Justice with a Second-Best Approach to the Insider–Outsider Problem," *Raisons Politiques* 73 (1), 61–82.

My 2013 book, *Independence, Propertylessness, and Basic Income*, laid out the indepentarian theory of freedom as "Effective Control Self-Ownership" ("ECSO" or for clarity, "ECSO freedom") the effective power to accept or refuse active cooperation with other willing people. It argued that one of the institutions necessary to protect ECSO freedom was some form of Basic Income Guarantee (BIG) at least large enough to meet people's basic needs.

BIG is an unconditional income floor, below which no one's income can fall for any reason. Universal Basic Income (UBI) is one form of BIG; it establishes the income floor by providing an unconditional income to everyone regardless of their private income. Other forms of BIG establish that floor by providing income only to those whose private income falls below a certain amount. I usually use the term UBI because is my preferred model of BIG, but none of the arguments in this book are specific to UBI.[7]

Respect for ECSO freedom puts one significant constraint on any political-economic system, but it says little about what forms of property are otherwise justifiable.[8] This book presents the first tentative statement of JPA property theory. It addresses and rejects natural-rights-based arguments for highly unequal private property systems like the one we have (Chapters 2–5). It then discusses the JPA alternative, the approximation of a property-rights accord (Chapter 6). It argues that taxes and regulations should be considered part of the purchase price of a good. People who wish to control, use, or use up external assets need to pay the costs that one person's control over anything made out of natural resources imposes on people who have to make do without those resources and who are affected by the environmental impact of its production and use. The solution involves the attempt to get a majority of people to agree on whether, how many, and which resources to privatize and on what terms: price, length of tenure, regulations, and so on. I argue that the solution must include the highest sustainable BIG that can be derived from the portion of assets that are privatized both to bring less advantaged people into agreement and to compensate dissenters.

[7] Widerquist, Karl (Forthcoming). *Universal Basic Income: Essential Knowledge*. Cambridge, MA: MIT Press.

[8] Widerquist, *Property and the Power*.

The conclusion (Chapter 7) discusses how to harmonize the two very different arguments for BIG in this book and in *Independence, Propertylessness, and Basic Income* (the two parts of my 2006 dissertation).[9]

The theory presented here is part of a larger project to develop JPA theory. Therefore, it has some relationship to the works below. I try to cite them when relevant.

The following books and articles explain, elaborate, argue for, and apply the indepentarian theory of ECSO freedom: "The Physical Basis of Voluntary Trade" (2010), "Why we Demand an Unconditional Basic Income: the ECSO freedom case" (2011), and *Independence, Propertylessness, and Basic Income* (2013).[10] The article, "Reciprocity and the Guaranteed Income" (1999)[11] defends BIG against the objection that it violates the principle of "reciprocity" by taking the offense: it argues that the background system of property rights without BIG violates reciprocity. In so doing, it makes an embryonic statement of the theory I am still trying to develop into JPA.

The following articles further elaborate JPA property theory: "A Permanent Endowment for the United States" (2012), "Why Link Basic Income to Resource Taxation?" (2012), "The People's Endowment" (2016).[12]

The following books and articles explain the need for JPA theory and/or criticize competing theories: "A Dilemma for Libertarianism" (2009), *Prehistoric Myths in Modern Political Philosophy* (2017), "My

[9] Ibid.

[10] Widerquist, Karl (2008). "The Physical Basis of Voluntary Trade." *Human Rights Review* 11 (1): 83–103; Widerquist, Karl (2011). "Why We Demand an Unconditional Basic Income: The ECSO Freedom Case." In *Arguing about Justice: Essays for Philippe Van Parijs*. Axel Gosseries and Yannick Vanderborght (eds.). Louvain-la-Neuve, Belgium: Presses universitaires de Louvain, 387–394; Widerquist, *Independence*.

[11] Widerquist, Karl (1999). "Reciprocity and the Guaranteed Income." *Politics and Society* 33: 386–401.

[12] Widerquist, Karl (2012). "A Permanent Endowment for the United States," In *Exporting the Alaska Model: Adapting the Permanent Fund Dividend for Reform Around the World*, Widerquist, Karl and Michael W. Howard (eds.). New York: Palgrave Macmillan, 163–167; Michael W. Howard and Karl Widerquist (2012). "Why Link Basic Income to Resource Taxation?" In *Alaska's Permanent Fund Dividend: Examining Its Suitability as a Model*, Karl Widerquist and Michael W. Howard (eds.). New York: Palgrave Macmillan, 205–220; Karl Widerquist (2016). "The People's Endowment." In *Institutions for Future Generations*. Axel Gosseries and Inigo Gonzalez (eds.). Oxford University Press, 312–330;

Own Private Basic Income" (2018), "The Pursuit of Accord: Toward a Theory of Justice With a Second-Best Approach to the Insider–Outsider Problem" (2019), "Why Private Property?" (2019), *the Prehistory of Private Property: Implications for Modern Political Theory* (2021), "The State of Nature, Prehistory, and Mythmaking" (2022).[13]

These articles reply to potential objections to indepentarian theory and policy: "Reciprocity and the Guaranteed Income" (1999), "Who Exploits Who?" (2006), "Does She Exploit or Doesn't She?" (2005).[14]

My forthcoming book, *Universal Basic Income: Essential Knowledge*, presents (among other things) some indepentarian ideas for a lay audience.[15]

And the dissertation that this book is drawn from is *Property and the Power to Say no: A Freedom-Based Argument for Basic Income.*[16]

[13] Widerquist, Karl (2009). "A Dilemma for Libertarianism," *Politics, Philosophy, and Economics* 8 (1): 43–72; Widerquist, Karl and Grant McCall (2017). *Prehistoric Myths in Modern Political Philosophy.* Edinburgh: Edinburgh University Press; Widerquist, Karl (2018). "My Own Private Basic Income." In *It's Basic Income: the Global Debate*, Amy Downes and Stewart Lansley (eds.). Bristol, UK: Policy Press, 48–53; Widerquist, Karl. "The Pursuit of Accord"; Jean-Fabien Spitz, Hillel Steiner, Philippe Van Parijs and Karl Widerquist (2019). "Why Private Property?" *Raisons Politiques* 73 (1), 119–131; Widerquist, Karl and Grant S. McCall (2021). *The Prehistory of Private Property: Implications for Modern Political Theory*, Edinburgh: Edinburgh University Press; Widerquist, Karl and Grant S McCall (2022). "The State of Nature, Prehistory, and Mythmaking." In *The State of Nature: Histories of an Idea.* Anne Peters and Mark Somos (eds.). Brill Publishers, 399–421.

[14] Widerquist "Reciprocity"; Widerquist, Karl (2006). "Who Exploits Who?" *Political Studies* 54 (3): 444–464; Widerquist, Karl (2005). "Does She Exploit or Doesn't She?" In *The Ethics and Economics of the Basic Income Guarantee*, Karl Widerquist, Michael A. Lewis, and Steven Pressman (eds.). Aldershot, UK: Ashgate, 138–162.

[15] Widerquist, *Universal Basic Income.*

[16] Widerquist, *Property and the Power.*

CHAPTER 2

The Problem of Property

Seven stranded castaways live on an uncharted desert isle. Wealthy Mr. Howell asks working-class Gilligan to dig a hole for a barbeque pit. In doing so, Gilligan digs up a locked treasure chest. Before opening it, the two begin to dispute its ownership. Both apparently base their claims on Lockean unilateral appropriation: Gilligan mixed his labor with the chest (by cutting into the turf) and Mr. Howell mixed his servant's labor with the chest (by asking Gilligan to cut into the turf). They ask the wise Professor to act as judge in their dispute. In an ignorable breech of disinterest, the Professor rules that the chest belongs equally to all seven of the castaways, none of whom has special claim to the island's resources. Strong Skipper flings a rope over a high tree branch and hoists up the chest. Before he could drop it, greedy Mr. Howell, working within the legally ascribed egalitarian property-rights regime but not wanting to miss his chance to be the sole owner of the contents of the treasure chest, offers the other six castaways a large sum of money for the exclusive right to it. They decline; he raises his offer, and keeps raising it until all six of the other castaways agree to respect his ownership of the chest. Skipper drops the chest. It breaks open, revealing only worthless cannonballs, of which, the weeping Mr. Howell is now the undisputed owner.

—Elroy Schwartz (summarized)[1]

[1] Schwartz, E. and O. Crawford (1965). "Plant You Now, Dig You Later," CBS Television. This example is actually rather advanced, incorporating uncertainty and a prior distribution of wealth. Uncertainty complicates the issues I wish to discuss, but it does

K. Widerquist, *The Problem of Property*, Exploring the Basic Income Guarantee, https://doi.org/10.1007/978-3-031-21948-1_2

This book addresses the question of what property-rights regime delivers the most extensive equal liberty (understood as freedom from interference in the continuous, scalar, or incremental sense of the term as opposed to the dichotomous sense of freedom discussed in my earlier book[2]). The goal is to determine the property-rights regime that delivers the maximal freedom consistent with equal freedom for all. It rejects the concept of a natural right to property. The rights it argues for are derived from the goal of maximizing equal freedom in the neutral sense of the term. The theory of status freedom as ECSO freedom acts as a constraint on the property system, and so I'll mention it only when relevant.

This book argues the property-rights regime that delivers the maximal equal freedom requires the approximation of an accord. Under this regime, people obtain title to an unowned natural resource (or a product of past generations) by paying their contemporaries sufficiently so that it is in their interest to agree to respect their property rights. In other words, people can obtain an approximation of a property right in unowned external assets by making it in each other's interest to treat their holdings as property. Call it "as-if property." It argues (among other things) that private property requires some form of BIG if it is going to be consistent with maximal equal freedom.

This theory of the relationship between property and liberty runs counter to the argument from liberty for right-libertarianism.[3] I use

not change my conclusions, and so I will set it aside entirely. It is interesting, however, that the participants choose to make their decisions under uncertainty when they could easily have resolved the uncertainty first and distributed the property second. By a prior distribution of wealth, I mean that Mr. Howell is wealthy before the assignment of a property right to this external asset, whereas people usually talk about an initial assignment of property rights and subsequent trade. It would be easy to write the prior distribution of wealth out of the story: Mr. Howell possesses greater talent, skill, or willingness to work than anyone else. Instead of bidding for the treasure chest in cash, he offers a contract to provide services for everyone else.

[2] Widerquist, *Property and the Power*.

[3] Kagan, Shelly (1994). "The Argument From Liberty." In *In Harm's Way: Essays in Honor of Joel Feinberg*. Cambridge: Cambridge University Press, 16–41. I take the phrase, "argument from liberty," from Kagan but use it differently. He questions whether strong rights of any kind promote the greatest freedom from interference. I discuss whether strong *property* rights are consistent with the most extensive equal freedom.

"the argument from liberty" for any argument involving the claim that property rights established unilaterally over natural resources without compensation for, or consent of, the propertyless deliver the maximal equal freedom for all. "Right-libertarianism," is the belief that governments should have minimum or perhaps nonexistent powers to tax, regulate, or redistribute private property.[4] Right-libertarians might better be called "propertarians" or "property rights advocates" because, as argued below, they promote property rights for some at the expense of equal liberty for all.[5]

Many critics have conceded some or all of the argument from liberty to right-libertarianism. Isaiah Berlin, for example, argues that no matter how morally right or desirable redistribution from the propertied to the propertyless may be, it entails an absolute loss of liberty.[6] Thomas Scanlon states that Robert Nozick[7] adheres "as closely as possible to the idea that ... all valid obligations derive from consent."[8] Scanlon makes this remark despite recognizing that heritable property rights disadvantage the poor of subsequent generations without their consent[9]—an obligation which (he should also recognize) is nonconsensual.[10]

[4] Authors who make rights-based or liberty-based arguments for one version of right-libertarianism or another include: Von Mises, L. (1927). *Liberalism in the Classical Tradition*. Irvington, NY: The Foundation for Economic Education; Hayek, F. A. (1944). *The Road to Serfdom*. London: Routledge; Hayek, F. A. (1960). *The Constitution of Liberty*. Chicago: University of Chicago Press; Friedman M. (1962). *Capitalism and Freedom*. Chicago: University of Chicago Press; Nozick; Friedman M. and R. Friedman (1980). *Free to Choose: A Personal Statement*. New York: Harcourt Brace Jovanovich; Rothbard, Murray (1982). *The Ethics of Liberty*. Atlantic Highlands, NJ: Humanities Press; Narveson, J. (1988). *The Libertarian Idea*. Philadelphia: Temple University Press; Murray, C. A. (1997). *What it Means to be a Libertarian*. New York: Broadway Books.

[5] See also Widerquist, "Dilemma;" Widerquist and McCall, *Prehistoric Myths*; Widerquist and McCall, *The Prehistory of Private Property*.

[6] Berlin, Isaiah I. (1969). *Four Essays on Liberty*. Oxford: Oxford University Press, 125.

[7] Nozick, R. (1974). *Anarchy, State, and Utopia*. New York: Basic Books, Inc.

[8] Scanlon, Thomas T. (1981). "Nozick on Rights, Liberty, and Property." In *Reading Nozick: Essays on Anarchy, State, and Utopia*. Oxford: Basil Blackwell, 107–130, 107.

[9] Ibid., 110–111.

[10] See Chapter 4; Widerquist, *Property and the Power*; Widerquist and McCall, *The Prehistory of Private Property*; Cohen, G. A. (1995). *Self-Ownership, Freedom, and Equality*. Cambridge: Cambridge University Press

This chapter clarifies the issue of property to set the stage for my arguments against existing property theories and in favor of an alternative.

1 Assets, Property, and Ownership

A discussion of property rights or ownership rights has to begin with an understanding of what is being owned. I use the economists' definition of a "good" as anything a person values. It is whether it has market value or not. Goods do not have to be physical objects. Software, time, a beautiful sky, a day at the races, a night at the opera, friendship, free speech, and property rights are all goods. Goods can be categorized in many different ways, three of which are relevant to the discussion here.

Goods can be classified as "internal" and "external assets." "Internal assets" are the goods that make up part of a person's self, such as body parts, abilities, talents, thoughts, memories, and emotions. The concept of ECSO freedom proposed in my earlier book implies that individuals should have effective control over their internal assets.[11] "External assets" are all goods that are not a part of a person's self, including land and minerals, the things past or present generations have made out of land and minerals, knowledge left by previous generations, and so on.[12]

Goods can also be classified as "natural resources" and "finished products." Natural resources are all the products of nature, whether embedded in other goods or not. These include land, water, minerals, plant life, and so on. Finished products are goods that have been altered in the production process and are now in their final form, such as machine tools.

Goods can just as well be classified as "resources" and "consumption goods." Resources are goods that are used to produce other goods. They include natural resources such as land but also finished products such as machine tools. Consumption goods are goods that are used directly by consumers to fulfill their needs or wants but not to produce anything else for exchange with others. Consumption goods include many finished products, such as cars and paintings, but they also include raw natural resources that are enjoyed directly by consumers, such as a nature park or a sunset.

[11] Widerquist, *Property and the Power*.

[12] Van Parijs, P. (1995). Real Freedom for All: What (If Anything) Can Justify Capitalism? Oxford: Oxford University Press.

The word "property" is often used in three different ways. The first refers to any good that is owned. The second refers only to a subset of the first definition of property: external assets. The third refers to a smaller subset: external assets capable of generating income. People who do not have enough wealth to devote any of it to investment can be called propertyless, but by this definition, "propertyless" people might own a substantial amount of noninvestment property. I use property in all three ways, but I think the meaning in each case is clear from context. I also use the term "property rights" when it is important to distinguish between property as a good and as a set of rights over that good.

"Ownership" is a set of "incidents" (rights and duties) that a person can have over an asset. Anthony Honoré provides an excellent analysis of ownership in contemporary market economies. He focuses on "the liberal concept of full individual ownership," which he defines as, "the greatest possible interest in a thing which a mature system of law recognizes."[13]

According to Honoré, full liberal ownership constitutes the following eleven incidents:

1. The right to possess,
2. The right to use,
3. The right to manage (i.e. the right to decide how it is used and by whom),
4. The right to the income the property generates,
5. The right to capital (i.e. the right to transfer property to others or to consume, destroy, or waste it),
6. The right to security (i.e. the right to refuse involuntary transfers),
7. Transmissibility (the right to transfer it to heirs),
8. The absence of term (i.e. ownership is open-ended; it does not terminate until voluntarily transferred by the owner or their successors),
9. The duty to prevent harm (i.e. the duty not to manage one's property in a way that potentially harms another person or another person's property),
10. Liability to execution (i.e. that property may be seized by creditors, and *possibly* that it may be taxed or appropriated by the state), and

[13] Honoré, A. (1987). *Making Law Bind*. Oxford: Oxford University Press, 161–162.

11. Residuary character (i.e. eventually other interests in the property would become extinct to the benefit of the owner).[14]

According to Honoré, different political systems may extend ownership to more or fewer things, but they tend to define ownership similarly. Nearly every society that recognizes ownership of external assets recognizes these eleven incidents as full ownership, but these incidents do not constitute absolute ownership, which he does not attempt to define.[15] Many weaker forms of ownership also exist in most societies, including easements, short-term leases, partnerships, and use rights.

I use the term "strong property rights" for any property rights without the duty to attain the consent of (or provide compensation for) the propertyless, even though such rights could be somewhat weaker or stronger than Honoré's full liberal ownership. Honoré is unwilling to say whether taxation of property is a standard incident of full individual[16] ownership even though taxation is as common as property.[17] He does not discuss why full liberal ownership is such a common institution or whether it is justifiable.

Although the following point plays little part in the discussion here, readers should note that Honoré's list of incidents is culturally specific. Many peoples known to anthropology define rights over goods in ways that can't easily be described in terms of items on his list.[18]

Vallentyne, Steiner, and Otsuka make an observation that could help explain why full ownership is so common. They use a similar but streamlined list of rights (control, compensation, enforcement, transfer, and immunity to the nonconsensual loss) without including a list of duties.[19] They claim that ownership so defined is, "the *logically* strongest set of ownership rights over a thing that a person can have compatibly with others having such rights over everything else."[20] The authors are aware,

[14] Ibid., condensed and paraphrased from 166–175.

[15] Ibid., 163.

[16] Ibid., 175.

[17] Widerquist and McCall, *The Prehistory of Private Property*.

[18] Ibid.

[19] Vallentyne, P., H. Steiner and M. Otsuka (2005). "Why Left-Libertarianism is Not Incoherent, Indeterminate, or Irrelevant." *Philosophy and Public Affairs* 33 (2), 201–215.

[20] Ibid., 204.

however, that strong property rights are not the only possible way, or necessarily the most desirable way to define ownership.

The strongest set of property rights compatible with *someone* having such rights over everything else is not necessarily the same as the strongest set of property rights compatible with *everyone* having the most extensive equal freedom. For example, sovereign dictatorship is the most extensive right over a territory one person can have compatible with someone else having such rights over all other territories; yet it is clearly inconsistent with everyone (including people who aren't dictators) having the most extensive equal freedom. Is full liberal ownership of external assets (without compensation for, or consent of, the propertyless) consistent with equal freedom for all?

Too often, property rights advocates treat full ownership as if it is a fact of nature, unquestioningly accepting that property rights naturally must include all eleven of Honoré's incidents plus the freedom from taxation, but no such assumption can go unquestioned in a search for the greatest equal freedom for all people.

Property can be effectively unowned or held by an individual, group, or nation. Property rights can consist of any or all of these eleven incidents in any combination or something else entirely. For example, a confiscatory inheritance tax would eliminate transmissibility without eliminating the absence of term. Property could be held by individuals in long-term leases that eventually reverted to the state, giving the government the absence of term and the residuary character but giving the leaseholder all other incidents. Laws that regulate how a property can be used grant the state some of the right to manage. Property can be taxed to benefit the propertyless, which can be considered an increase in its liability to execution and the duty to prevent harm or a reduction of the right to the income the property generates. External assets could be governed by a set of common access rights held by everyone. A successful natural rights defense of property has to explain which of these incidents "naturally" adhere to property and why. This effort is lacking in most property-rights literature.

2 Rights to Property and Right-Libertarianism

No government follows the principles advocated by right-libertarian theorists, but I address their arguments because they provide the most extensive and explicit defenses of the familiar institution of full liberal ownership. Slightly weaker views of ownership are probably more common, such as the belief that strong property rights or nearly full ownership should require a duty to aid the poor, or the belief that full ownership is most consistent with freedom but other principles of justice, such as equality, override the freedom embodied in a system of strong private property rights. This book argues that full individual property rights without the consent of or compensation for the propertyless are inconsistent with liberty, and so the theory it puts forward involves no conflict between equality and freedom. It also argues that a duty to aid the poor is not enough to make full individual ownership consistent with the greatest equal freedom. I focus on the right-libertarian argument for full individual ownership with the understanding that my arguments apply as well to weaker forms of property than those advocated by right-libertarians.

For the purposes here, I define right-libertarianism as an ethical theory of property rights[21] to external assets that can be characterized by the following statements:

1. Property rights are natural, moral rights that exist independently of government through unilateral appropriation.
2. Property rights should constitute and do constitute full individual ownership as defined by Honoré.[22]
3. Taxes and government regulations on property constitute government interference with individual property rights.
4. Government is ethically bound to limit its interference with property rights to the minimum necessary to secure and protect the rights of property ownership and formal self-ownership.
5. The argument from liberty: a government that behaves in accordance with propositions 1–4 creates the most extensive liberty

[21] Other aspects of right- or left-libertarian theory are not a concern of this book.

[22] Honoré.

compatible with equal liberty for all (liberty understood in the continuous negative sense).[23]

The difference between the existing legal recognition of property rights and libertarianism is largely in point 4. The argument in this book is aimed at points 1, 2, and 3, and so it is aimed as much at the current legal system of property rights as it is at right-libertarianism. It does not argue that all private property is inconsistent with equal freedom but it argues that some forms of taxation, regulation, and redistribution of property are necessary to secure the greatest equal freedom for all. If that argument is successful, a coherent justification of full liberal ownership has to defend strong property rights *at the expense* of the most extensive equal freedom for all. There are non-liberty-based arguments for right-libertarianism, but few of them recognize that so-called right-libertarianism conflicts with the most extensive equal freedom for all or that strong property rights conflict with any consistent set of equal rights and are, therefore, best understood as legal privileges.

3 Special Rights, Legal Privileges, and Full Individual Ownership of Property

There is an important distinction between general rights arguments for property and special rights arguments for property.[24] A general right—such as free speech—is a right that everyone has. A special right is a right that arises in a particular situation. For example, if as repayment for a loan, Ginger promises to pay Skipper $100 a week, Skipper attains a special right that Gilligan does not possess. A further distinction can be made between special legal rights that do and do not constitute legal privileges. In the case above, Gilligan's right status does not change. He had a duty to respect someone else's right to property in that $100 before the transfer, and he continues to have the same duty after the transfer (although his relative wealth may have changed). By contrast, legal privileges provide special rights for one person by reducing the rights of or

[23] I discuss different conceptions of libertarianism more fully in Widerquist, Karl (2009). "Libertarianism." In *The International Encyclopedia of Public Policy: Governance in a Global Age, Volume 3*, Phillip O'Hara (ed.). Perth: GPERU.

[24] Waldron, J. (1988). *The Right*. Oxford: Clarendon Press, 116–117.

imposing duties on another without their consent or a similar right. For example, King A appoints subject B as the feudal lord of peasant C, giving C the obligation to perform ten hours per week of service for B. Legal privileges as such are inconsistent with equal freedom for all.

There are two kinds of cases in which a person can hold a special right without holding a legal privilege. First, a special right that necessarily follows from general rights extended to all is not a privilege. For example, the general right to liberty arguably implies the special right to a fair trial for those threatened with imprisonment after being accused of a crime. People whose general right to liberty is not under threat do not need a trial. Similarly, Skipper's special right to collect a debt from Ginger follows from the general right of people to lend things to each other.

Second, special rights are not legal privileges if they somehow increase the freedom of those who are underprivileged by them. For example, the most important and extensive freedoms of the least capable people might be best protected when only knowledgeable, well-trained, and disinterested judges have the right to settle legal disputes even if people without the requirements would like to hold that office.

Marriage is a special right that is not a legal privilege. Suppose Skipper and Ginger get married. Skipper obtains special legal rights that Gilligan does not have, and he takes away Gilligan's opportunity to wed Ginger, but the rule, *everyone has the right to have or refuse a marriage contract with another willing person*, is necessary to create the maximum freedom from interference with an individual's marriage decision compatible with equal freedom for all. Skipper's special right to wed Ginger follows from that general right applied to everyone. Out-competing someone in marriage or the market does not interfere with their rights status, even if it makes them worse off than they would have otherwise been.[25]

Any rule designed to give Gilligan greater opportunity to marry the person of his choice (assuming it is Ginger) would come at the expense of Ginger's opportunity to refuse an unwanted marriage, which is a more central and more important general right. Therefore, marriage is a special right that not everyone will be able to assume even if they want to, but it is not a privilege as long as everyone has the same legal right to obtain it, and it does not interfere (in an absolute sense) with people who cannot find a willing partner. Although Gilligan is worse off in the sense that

[25] Cohen, 227–228.

Ginger is no longer willing to make an agreement with him that she otherwise might have, his rights status does not change. He has a duty to respect the ECSO freedom (and other rights) of Skipper and Ginger whether or not they wed each other. Skipper's invitation is only one of an infinite number of reasons why Ginger might have decided not to accept Gilligan's offer. If we accept her prerogative to make that decision, Skipper's influence over that decision is none of Gilligan's business.

Does full individual ownership of external assets similarly maximize equal liberty? Nozick attempts to draw such an analogy.[26] It is easy to show that the trade of existing property rights is not a legal privilege, but the same cannot be said for the establishment, definition, and maintenance of any particular property system. Consider a rule such as *everyone has the right to trade external assets (in which they have legitimate title) with other willing people*. As in the above-example of the loan, the exchange of existing property rights does not affect the rights status of other parties in an absolute sense. A naïve justification of property would stop here, as Nozick's does. People acquire property through voluntary trade; we can see that trade is not a legal privilege, because it resembles the voluntary decision to marry. Therefore, interference with property interferes with freedom. But the analogy does not hold. Trade is not the *source* of property.

Justification of the exchange of property, once defined, does not justify property itself or explain why property must be defined as full individual ownership rather than some weaker bundle of rights. Trade merely exchanges titles, and it cannot occur until the legal authority has already recognized (or established) the relevant property titles.[27] The issues of how assets became property and what rights owners have over assets are more important to the propertyless than the exchange of property. Many complaints about the power of owners are misdirected at the market for trading the titles that the legal system has created.

To examine whether property rights are special rights or legal privileges, it is necessary to examine the source of those rights, which in most

[26] Nozick, 262–263.

[27] Ibid., 72. Cohen in turn refers to Marx, K. (1978). *Capital, Vol. III*. Middlesex: Harmondsworth, 911; and H. Spencer (1872). *Social Statics*. New York: D. Appleton and Company, 115. Similar observations have been made by Rousseau, J.-J. (1984). *A Discourse in Inequality*. New York: Penguin Classics, 109; Paine, T. (1797). *Agrarian Justice*. Philadelphia: R. Folwell, for Benjamin Franklin Bache; and many others.

property theories, is a supposed principle of unilateral appropriation. That is, one person takes unowned natural resources and makes them private property without the consent of anyone else. Does a right of unilateral appropriation, such as *everyone has the right to appropriate property, if they can find unowned property to appropriate*, create the most extensive freedom compatible with equal freedom for all? Is it a special right or a legal privilege?

Suppose, instead of interacting with a person named Ginger, Skipper appropriates a piece of property on Ginger Avenue. Unlike exchanges, this unilateral action interferes with Gilligan, who now can make no use of the Ginger Avenue lot without Skipper's permission. Gilligan may neither appropriate the lot individually nor use it as common property, as he was free to do when it was unowned. The crucial difference between the person named Ginger and the property on Ginger Avenue is that the property has no will of its own to be interfered with. No matter how much you might love your property, your property will never love you back. Ginger's status as a free person was crucial to the marriage story, but the property on Ginger Avenue has no such status to be interfered with. The only relevant parties are Skipper and Gilligan. Skipper's appropriation increases his freedom to act and interferes with Gilligan's freedom to act by imposing duties on Gilligan that did not exist before.

Rights and duties to a particular resource are equal when the resource is unowned and unequal when it is owned by one person and not another. This observation implies difficulty in reconciling unequal ownership with the greatest equal freedom for all. But that reconciliation is not necessarily impossible. If *everyone* had the opportunity to appropriate property, and uses of appropriated property were more important than the uses of unowned or collectively held property, appropriation would be a special right that follows from a general right. However, if resources are scarce (i.e., if there are fewer available than everyone would like to appropriate), it is impossible to extend full ownership rights to appropriated property *and* give everyone the same right to appropriate property.

There can be no general right to appropriate scarce resources. Some people have no opportunity to appropriate property, not because they are unable to do so, but because all resources have been appropriated and property is protected by legal force. Government interference, in the form of establishing and protecting special rights to property, is the reason the propertyless are excluded from making any use of external assets.

The duties imposed on others by appropriation make property a very different sort of special right than a marriage contract or the right of a free trial. Jeremy Waldron argues that the imposition of potentially onerous duties without consent makes appropriation inconsistent with nearly any other duty people are expected to accept.[28] Unless the appropriation of property does something for the propertyless, ownership is a legal privilege and not a right.

If the appropriated property is defended by the state without the consent of the propertyless, a principle that has nothing to do with voluntary exchange between individuals comes between an individual and access to natural resources. Gerald Cohen calls this a "banal truth." That is, "if the state prevents me from doing something that I want to do, then it places a restriction on my freedom."[29] The banality of his truth is not a new observation,[30] but it must nevertheless be stated because so many right-libertarians ignore it. Waldron[31] quotes Kant as recognizing this fact, "When I declare (by word or deed), 'I will that an external thing shall be mine,' I thereby declare it obligatory for everyone else to refrain from using the object of my will. This is an obligation that no one would have apart from this juridical act of mine."[32] Wenar describes it especially well:

> Before acquisition [his word for appropriation], each inhabitant of the state of nature may use, consume, damage or destroy anything, just as she likes. After acquisition, every person but the acquirer has a duty not to disturb the acquired thing without the acquirer's permission. The acquirer in exercising her acquisitive right imposes a duty on each non-acquirer with respect to the acquired thing, and without any non-acquirer's consent. By the exercise of the acquisitive right, the acquirer unilaterally imposes duties on everyone else. Moreover, the acquirer typically imposes these duties intending only her own advantage, and since they are strong duties, they may be burdensome to those who bear them.[33]

[28] Waldron, *The Right*, 168–172, 271–283.

[29] Cohen, 55.

[30] Rousseau.

[31] Waldron, *The Right*, 266.

[32] Kant, I. (1965). *The Metaphysical Elements of Justice*. Indianapolis: Bobbs Merill, 64.

[33] Wenar, L. (1998). "Original Acquisition of Private Property." *Mind* 107 (428), 799–820, 806.

Cheyney Ryan argues, based on similar reasoning, that if we adopt extensive property rights, "it is because we treasure some freedoms more than others" not because property rights are unambiguously associated with greater freedom.[34] The argument below goes further: full or strong ownership rights do not merely promote one type of freedom for everyone at the expense of another type of freedom for everyone; they promote the freedom of some people at the expense of reducing the very same freedoms for others. That is, they promote privilege at the expense of maximal equal freedom for all.

If this argument against strong property rights is to be successful, it must overcome the Lockean and right-libertarian arguments that property owners have done something (following from equal freedom) that justifies their claims to property. The following three chapters examine Lockean and right-libertarian justifications for unilateral appropriation and full ownership to show that they have failed to establish property in a way that would be consistent with equal freedom for all.

[34] Ryan, C. C. (1981). "Yours, Mine, and Ours: Property Rights and Individual Liberty." In *Reading Nozick: Essays on Anarchy, State, and Utopia*, J. Paul (ed.) Oxford: Basil Blackwell, 323–343, 340; McCloskey, H. J. (1965). "A Critique of the Ideals of Liberty." *Mind* 74; and Sidgwick, H. (1966). *The Methods of Ethics*. New York: Dover Publications.

CHAPTER 3

Lockean Property Theory: A Menu of Options for the Justification of Unilateral Appropriation

This chapter is a summary of "Lockean Theories of Property: Justifications for Unilateral Appropriation," which was published in *Public Reason* in 2010.[1]

I understood each and every word you said but not the order in which they appeared.

—William Haefeli[2]

Although John Locke's property theory, especially his principle of unilateral appropriation,[3] is undoubtedly influential, no one seems to agree on exactly what he was trying to say. He has been interpreted in so many strikingly different ways[4] that there is unlikely to be an "a-ha" moment, when someone writes *the* interpretation, effectively ending the controversy. Given the influence of and the controversy over Locke's theory of unilateral appropriation, it is worthwhile to take stock of the range of theories that have been developed out of it. In that effort, this

[1] Widerquist, "Lockean Theories."

[2] Haefeli, William (1999). "New Yorker Cartoon," *The New Yorker*, August 2, 1999.

[3] LockeLocke, John J. (1960 [1690]). *Two Treatises of Government*. Cambridge: Cambridge University Press, especially *Second Treatise*, Chapter 5.

[4] Widerquist, "Lockean Theories."

K. Widerquist, *The Problem of Property*, Exploring the Basic Income Guarantee, https://doi.org/10.1007/978-3-031-21948-1_3

chapter presents a critical examination of Locke and his interpreters point-by-point, not to identify the one correct interpretation of his theory but to identify the menu of options: the range of potentially valid ways in which unilateral appropriation might be used to justify private property rights.[5]

This menu is most valuable to opponents, because, although supporters only need to pick the one version they find most plausible, anyone claiming to refute the appropriation-based justification of property rights must address all potentially valid versions of it on the menu. Therefore, my attention is not limited to interpretations of *Locke's* theory; it also includes *Lockean* extensions and modifications. I use "Locke's theory" to refer to Locke's own ideas and "Lockean theory" to refer to any theory somehow based on Locke or unilateral appropriation.[6] The goal of this chapter is to identify the range of plausible appropriation-based justifications of private property. Issues of why Locke said what he said, what his real intentions were, or how one comes up with a particular interpretation of Locke are of only secondary relevance.

This article is organized as follows. Section 1 discusses appropriation in the state of nature. Section 2 discusses whether and how many "Lockean provisos" should be attached to the appropriation principle. Section 3 discusses how the proviso can be fulfilled in a world of scarce resources. Section 4 discusses the transition from a theory of appropriation in the state of nature to a theory of property in civil society. Section 5 concludes by putting together the menu of options—an outline of Lockean property theory—and shows how various interpretations and reformulations of appropriation theory can be understood as specifications of that menu.

1 Appropriation in the State of Nature

Locke begins in a state of nature that has abundant common resources but lacks government, money, trade, and abundant resources available for appropriation. He defends an appropriation principle by which the first person to mix their labor with land needs no one else's consent to

[5] Widerquist, "Lockean Theories."

[6] Sreenivasan, 106.

privatize it.[7] A farmer (who alters the land through labor) appropriates it; a hunter (who labors on land supposedly without altering it) does not.

Locke presents at least five possible justifications for appropriation. First, self-ownership implies a person owns their labor and any unowned thing they mix with it.[8] Second, labor accounts for most of the value of property,[9] because unimproved resources have little or no value.[10] Third, Laborers deserve the benefits of their efforts.[11] Fourth, improving resources effectively makes more resources available for others.[12] Fifth, appropriators have a right to produce their own subsistence.[13]

All of Locke's justifications for labor-based appropriation have been challenged by scholars.[14] Many authors have remarked that this argument justifies ownership of only the value added by the appropriator, not including the full resource value of an asset.[15]

Not all appropriation theorists accept first labor as the most plausible appropriation criterion, replacing it with the first claim, first use, first possession, or discovery.[16] Some have proposed additional justifications for appropriation, including that property takes a pivotal role

[7] Locke, §26–31, "§" refers to section (paragraph) numbers in Locke.

[8] Locke, §27–28.

[9] Locke, §28.

[10] Arneil, Barbara (1994). "Trade, Plantations, and Property: John Locke and the Economic Defense of Colonialism." *Journal of the History of Ideas* 55 (4): 591–609, 602; Olivecrona, Karl (1991 [1974]). "Locke's Theory of Appropriation." In *John Locke: Critical Assessments*, Richard Ashcraft (ed.). New York: Routledge, 327–342, 341; Cohen.

[11] Locke, §34; Becker, Lawrence C. (1977). *Property Rights: Philosophic Foundations*. London: Routledge and Kegan Paul, 35–36; Buckle, S. (1991). *Natural Law and the Theory of Property*. Oxford: Oxford University Press, 149–161.

[12] Locke, §37; Schmidtz, David. (1990). "When is Original Appropriation Required?" *The Monist*, October, 504–518; Schmidtz, David (1991). *The Limits of Government: An Essay on the Public Goods Argument*. Oxford: Westview Press, 17–24.

[13] Locke, §28–29.

[14] Waldron, J., *The Right*, 168–174; Sreenivasan, G. (1995). *The Limits of Lockean Rights in Property*. New York: Oxford University Press, 28–29.

[15] Epstein, Richard A. (1995). *Simple Rules for a Complex World*. Cambridge, MA: Harvard University Press, 60.

[16] Otsuka, Michael (2003). *Libertarianism without Inequality*. Oxford: Oxford University Press, 21 n. 29; Narveson, *The Libertarian Idea*, Chapter 7; Epstein; Kirzner, Israel M. (1989). *Discovery, Capitalism, and Distributive Justice*. Oxford: B. Blackwell, 18–19, 98–100.

in a person's life,[17] that a stable property rights system produces efficiency gains that benefit everyone,[18] and that appropriation is necessary to pursue projects.[19]

2 Three Provisos in One

No-waste: Locke argues that an appropriator must not waste their property or take more than they can use.[20] In the state of nature, this proviso ensures substantial equality by limiting the size of holdings to the amount a person can work directly, but it might have been a rationalization for the expansion of upper-class property rights through the enclosure movement in Britain and colonization abroad.[21]

Charity: Locke believed in a strong duty of charity by which everyone is entitled to maintain subsistence,[22] but scholars do not agree whether he includes charity as a proviso in his property theory.[23] If Locke intended

[17] Waldron, J. (1992). "Superseding Historic Injustice." *Ethics* 103 (1): 4–28.

[18] Epstein.

[19] Sanders, John T. (1987). "Justice and the Initial Acquisition of Property." *Harvard Journal of Law and Public Policy* 10: 367–399, 392–399; Lomasky, L. (1987). *Persons, Rights, and the Moral Community*. Oxford: Oxford University Press, 130–131.

[20] Locke, §31, §38, §46.

[21] Arneil; Arneil, Barbara (1996). *John Locke and America: The Defence of English Colonialism*. Oxford: Clarendon Press; Glausser, Wayne (1990). "Three Approaches to Locke and the Slave Trade." *Journal of the History of Ideas* 51 (2): 199–216; Olivecrona, Karl (1974). "Appropriation in the State of Nature: Locke on the Origin of Property." *Journal of the History of Ideas* 35 (2): 211–230, 592; Lebovics, Herman. (1991 [1986]). "The Uses of America in Locke's Second Treatise of Government." In *John Locke: Critical Assessments*, Richard Ashcraft (ed.). New York: Routledge, 254–284; for summary of the debate, see Widerquist, "Lockean Theories," 7–8; see also Widerquist and McCall, *The Prehistory of Private Property*, 148–150, 152–154, 240–257.

[22] Locke, §42. Dunn, John (1991 [1968]). "Justice and the Interpretation of Locke's Political Theory." In *John Locke: Critical Assessments*, Richard Ashcraft (ed.). New York: Routledge, 43–63.

[23] Sanders, 371–373; Waldron, J. (2002). *God, Locke, and Equality: Christian Foundations of John Locke's Political Thought*. Cambridge: Cambridge University Press, 177–185; Ashcraft, Richard. (1994). "Locke's Political Philosophy." In *The Cambridge Companion to Locke*, Vere Chappell (ed.). Cambridge: Cambridge University Press, 243, 226–251; Lamb, Robert, and Benjamin Thompson. (2009). "The Meaning of Charity in Locke's Political Thought." *European Journal of Political Theory* 8: 229–252.

a charity proviso, it was merely a paternal responsibility of the property-owning class rather than a challenge to the concentration of ownership. Locke may have believed, as many right-libertarians do, that redistributive taxation is seldom necessary because the market provides enough jobs for the able-bodied, and voluntary charity provides enough support for the infirm.[24]

Enough and as Good: Locke states that appropriation is valid, "at least where there is enough, and as good left in common for others,"[25] and he elaborates this idea significantly over several paragraphs.[26] Nozick calls this limitation "*the* Lockean proviso."[27] It has inspired diverse interpretation, beginning with Locke's placement of the words "at least." Seemingly, either the words "at least" mean nothing, or the entire proviso means nothing, in the sense that there are some unspecified cases in which a person can appropriate without leaving enough and as good for others.

Some scholars argue that Locke didn't intend the sufficiency limitation as a proviso at all. It could be a sufficient (but not necessary) condition for appropriation or merely a description of the effect of the no-waste proviso in the state of nature.[28] This interpretation has two difficulties. First, enough and as good cannot be successfully employed as a sufficient condition for appropriation.[29] Second, Locke does not state the proviso merely as a matter of fact but as a justification for appropriation. He repeatedly uses words like "injury," "complaint," "prejudice," and "intrench" seemingly to demonstrate that the enough and as good proviso justifies property *because* it ensures the appropriator "does as good as take nothing at all."[30] Why would Locke state this clause at all, and

[24] Waldron, *The Right*, 161; Winfrew, John C. (1991 [1981]). "Charity Versus Justice in Locke's Theory of Property." In *John Locke: Critical Assessments*, Richard Ashcraft (ed.). New York: Routledge, 384–401, 398.

[25] Locke, §27.

[26] Locke, §27–36.

[27] Nozick, 178–182.

[28] Thomson, Judith Jarvis (1976). "Property Acquisition." *Journal of Philosophy* 73: 664–666; Waldron (1979), 322; Waldron, *The Right*, 210–211; Waldron, *God, Locke, and Equality*, 172.

[29] Kramer, Matthew H. (2004). *John Locke and the Origins of Private Property*. Cambridge: Cambridge University Press, 106.

[30] Locke, §27–36.

return to it repeatedly in such strong terms, if he did not intend it as a proviso?

Some more extreme property rights advocates argue that appropriation theory is logically stronger without any provisos. They claim people have no positive right to resources. Therefore, other people's appropriation leaves them no worse off in terms of the rights they hold.[31] Opponents of this extreme view argue that without a proviso, appropriation interferes with, and therefore harms, anyone who is capable of using unappropriated resources.[32] If Locke did not intend the sufficiency limitation as a proviso, perhaps he should have. Probably because any justification of property seems weak and unpersuasive without it, most authors agree the enough and as good proviso is the most important limitation in Lockean property theory.[33] If the phrase "at least" is carefully placed, it could mean that when goods are not scarce, the appropriator is required either to compensate the non-appropriators or to obtain consent.[34]

With minor simplification, all three provisos can be combined into one by assuming that they all stem from the belief that people should be free to use resources to meet their needs. If we use the no-waste proviso as an instrument to help fulfill the others (even though this might not be Locke's intention) and assume that everyone is capable of providing for themselves given enough resources (perhaps by reselling them), we can treat the three as one without too much loss of generality. This combined proviso is somewhat broader than Nozick's characterization of sufficiency as "the" proviso.

3 Fulfilling the Proviso

This section discusses three questions about how the proviso should be fulfilled. Locke did not elaborate on these issues. Therefore, this discussion mostly involves Lockean adaptations.

[31] Kirzner, *Discovery*, 98–100; Narveson, *The Libertarian Idea*, 100–101; Rothbard, 244–45.

[32] Wenar.

[33] Sreenivasan, 40; Nozick.

[34] Sreenivasan, 40; Nozick; Tully, J. (1980). *A Discourse on Property: John Locke and His Adversaries*. Cambridge: Cambridge University Press.

3.1 *Must the Proviso Be Fulfilled in Resources or is Compensation Acceptable?*

It is unclear whether "enough and as good" should be left in the same kind of resources taken by the appropriator or whether the appropriator can replace natural resources with something else. Depending on the strength of the proviso, in-kind fulfillment might be difficult or impossible in a world with a population in the billions, but as long as production creates value, the possibility exists to fulfill the proviso by replacement or compensation. Locke seems to have had something like this in mind.[35] Whether he did or not, it seems like the logical extension of the proviso, and many Lockean authors make it explicit.[36] Three candidates for replacement—market opportunities, government services, and cash—play a part in the discussion below.

3.2 *Should the Proviso Be Fulfilled in Terms of Standard-of-Living or Independent Functioning?*

A living standard conception determines fulfillment of the proviso by comparing consumption levels of modern workers and people who lived before the establishment of agriculture.[37] This characterization allows people to claim that the proviso is fulfilled for a starving or malnourished person who owns a cell phone because cell phones have infinite cost in the state of nature. The characterization also ignores the important issue that appropriation reduces the freedom from interference of the propertyless and effectively forces them to participate in the market economy as a subordinate laborer.[38]

The independent functioning characterization of the proviso is that it should provide people direct and unconditional access to the level of independent functioning they could get with direct access to resources.

[35] Locke, §36, §41; Snyder, David C. (1991 [1986]). "Locke on Natural Law and Property Rights." In *John Locke: Critical Assessments*, Richard Ashcraft (ed.). New York: Routledge, 362–384, 374.

[36] Otsuka; Paine; Sreenivasan.

[37] Mack, E. (1995). "The Self-Ownership Proviso: A New and Improved Lockean Proviso." *Social Philosophy and Policy* 12: 186–218; Nozick (1974), 182.

[38] Carter, Alan (1989). *The Philosophical Foundations of Property Rights*. London: Harvester Wheatsheaf, 46; Bogart, J. H. (1985). "Lockean Provisos and State of Nature Theories." *Ethics* 95 (4): 828–836, 833–834; Widerquist, *Property and the Power*.

But the question of how the proviso is to be fulfilled is entirely separate from its level. His argument for nondependence is actually a call to fulfill the proviso in terms of independent functioning rather than the standard of living.

Tully and Sreenivasan argue that Locke saw the proviso as ensuring that the able-bodied have direct access to the means of production so that they do not become dependent proletarians,[39] which says something both about *how* the proviso should be fulfilled and about *how strong* it should be (see below). A. J. Simmons calls this idea non-dependence. Otsuka calls it "robust self-ownership." I call it independence, ECSO freedom, and basic autonomy.[40] If independent functioning is important (at any strength), market opportunities cannot fulfill the proviso. It requires compensation in cash or in goods and services.

This conception was not Locke's intent; he accepted the legitimacy of dependent wage labor,[41] probably believing that competition among employers gave workers sufficient freedom. Eric Mack explicitly uses that argument to reject concern for an independent functioning conception of the proviso.[42]

3.3 How Strong Should the Proviso Be?

The section identifies several different versions of the proviso in terms of its strength—i.e., the level or amount of compensation it requires.

The "weak" version, favored by Nozick, allows appropriators to privatize as long as everyone else is as well off as they would be if *no one* had appropriated any property and society remained in a state of nature.[43]

The "strong" version, identified by Nozick[44] but favored by Waldron, Sreenivasan, and Tully, allows appropriation as long as an equal share

[39] Tully; Sreenivasan.

[40] Simmons, A. J. (1992). *The Lockean Theory of Rights*. Princeton: Princeton University Press; Otsuka; Widerquist, *Property and the Power*.

[41] Waldron, *The Right*; Macpherson, C. B. (1962). *The Political Theory of Possessive Individualism: Hobbes to Locke*. Oxford: Clarendon Press, 216–217.

[42] Mack, "The Self-Ownership Proviso."

[43] Nozick, 178–179.

[44] Nozick, 174–182.

of the value of unimproved natural resources is available to everyone.[45] This version allows for inequality only in the improvements that have been made to resources. It can be fulfilled by taxing raw resource value at the highest sustainable rate and distributing the revenue equally to everyone.[46] Locke implies this equal shares version at one point writing, "He that had as good left for his improvement, *as was already taken up*, needed not complain."[47]

Both of these versions of the proviso could conceivably be fulfilled in terms of independent functioning without securing independence if one supposes that the living provided by that amount of resource access is not one that would provide an acceptable exit option from subordinate wage labor. I'll use the term "extra-strong" proviso for a version that secures a level of independent functioning high enough to maintain ECSO freedom.[48]

What I call the "maximum-strength" version of the proviso demands that everyone is entitled to access to as many resources as they can make use of. This version's strength is maximal, because under scarcity, each person can make use of more than a per capita share of resources, and in a monetary economy, there are few limits to how much a person can use.[49] The maximum-strength proviso would allow appropriation only of economically abundant goods, which have a market value of zero.

One might be tempted to think that there is no need for property when goods are abundant, but in Locke's state of nature, only raw resources are abundant, not finished products.[50] A sculptor can pick up a worthless rock by the side of a road and carve it into something valuable and scarce, even though abundant unimproved rocks remain. Under such conditions, someone who demands that particular rock clearly desires "the benefit of another's pains."[51] Locke relies on the maximum-strength proviso to justify property when resources are abundant, and implies it

[45] Sreenivasan, 40; Tully, 137–138; Waldron, *The Right*, 214–215.

[46] Steiner, Hillel (2009). "Left Libertarianism and the Ownership of Natural Resources." *Public Reason* 1 (1): 1–8, especially 5–6.

[47] Locke, §34, emphasis added.

[48] Widerquist, *Independence*.

[49] Locke, §45–50.

[50] Locke, §28.

[51] Locke, §34.

more often than he implies the strong or weak version. Only this version fully supports his claims of no "injury," "entrenchment," "prejudice," or "cause for complaint."[52]

Although the maximum-strength proviso has plausibility, it lacks applicability, because it justifies property only in abundant resources. Most authors who reject "the proviso" on the grounds that it is unfulfillable seem to have the maximum-strength version in mind.[53] Although several scholars have interpreted the proviso as an abundance condition,[54] I know of no explicit discussion of the difference between it and the equal shares version, and no discussion that both recognizes Locke's reliance on it in the state of nature and explains the move to the so-called "strong" version under scarcity.[55] However, some arguments in Lockean literature might be put to that purpose.

One option is to argue that the propertyless are not entitled to all they can appropriate now given current technology but only to all they would have been able to appropriate in the state of nature. Mack argues, "if the whole process of privatization leaves Sally with 'enough and as good' to use as she would have enjoyed (at a comparable cost) had all extra-personal resources remained in common, Sally will have no complaint."[56] Alan Ryan writes, "since all men have profited by entering a market society, there is no cause for complaint if some men have done better than others."[57]

This argument seems to be what Locke was getting at,[58] but it has three difficulties. First, it relies on the dubious empirical assumption that

[52] Locke, §27–36.

[53] Kirzner, *Discovery*, 156; Sartorius, Rolf (1984). "Persons and Property." In *Utility and Rights*, R. G. Frey (ed.). Minneapolis: University of Minnesota Press, 196–214, especially 210; Schmidtz, "When is Original Appropriation Required?", 504.

[54] Carter, 19.

[55] The closest I've found is Waldron, J. (2002). *God, Locke, and Equality: Christian Foundations of John Locke's Political Thought*. Cambridge: Cambridge University Press.

[56] Mack, Eric (2002). "Self-Ownership, Marxism, and Egalitarianism: Part II: Challenges to the Self-Ownership Thesis." *Politics, Philosophy & Economics* 1 (2): 237–76, 248; Sanders, 385 makes a similar argument.

[57] Ryan, Alan (1991 [1965]). "Locke and the Dictatorship of the Bourgeoisie." In *John Locke: Critical Assessments*, edited by Richard Ashcraft, 419–437. New York: Routledge, 433.

[58] Locke, §37–41.

everyone is better off now than every single person was before the invention of agriculture—a claim I've argued is false.[59] Second, it gives current property owners credit for all civilization's accomplishments. Third, as Michael Otsuka argues, the spirit of Locke's proviso is that one person's appropriation must not put another person at any disadvantage. Therefore, it must take into account everything non-appropriators might have done with resources, including taking the advantages current property holders have taken or creating a system that shares access to advantage more equally.[60]

There are several other possible ways to justify moving to a weaker proviso under scarcity. Right-libertarians could appeal to a finders-keepers ethic.[61] Left-libertarians could argue that the strong version best expresses the value of equal freedom from interference.[62] Liberal-egalitarians could argue that the proviso implies entitlement to a decent share of society's productive capacity.[63] Another option, explored in the next section, is to rely on a social agreement after the transition to civil society.

4 Property in Civil Society

Only the last few paragraphs of Locke's property chapter focus on civil society when three changes mark the transition: resource abundance ends, a monetary economy appears, and a government is established.[64] At times Locke seems to appeal to consent as the justification for property in civil society; at others, he seems to believe that ownership is not the sort of thing that requires consent.[65] My article argues that it is difficult to make any consistent interpretation of the role of consent in Locke's property theory, discusses the many different sides in the literature over it, and

[59] Widerquist and McCall, *Prehistoric Myths.*

[60] Otsuka, 24–26.

[61] Kirzner, *Discovery*, 16–18; Schmidtz, "When is Original Appropriation Required?" 511.

[62] Steiner, H. (1981). "Liberty and Equality." *Political Studies* 29: 555–569.

[63] Lemos, Ramon M. (1991 [1975]). "Locke's Theory of Property." In *John Locke: Critical Assessments*, Richard Ashcraft (ed.). New York: Routledge, 343–361.

[64] Locke, §45–51.

[65] Rapaczynski, Andrzej (1981). "Locke's Conception of Property and the Principle of Sufficient Reason." *Journal of the History of Ideas* 42 (2): 305–15, 306.

shows that scholars have proposed at least three different interpretations of what happens to property rights in Locke's transition to civil society[66]:

1. Property owners lose their natural property rights and receive whatever rights civil society agrees on.[67]
2. Money (somehow) allows unequal property rights to exist, but the propertyless maintain their rights under the proviso (s).[68]
3. The propertyless give up all or most of their rights under the proviso (s).[69]

Another important issue for the transition is the contention that Lockean theory can, at best, show how property *could have* arisen justly, but that doesn't necessarily make it relevant to actual, existing property rights, which cannot be traced by a series of just steps to original appropriation but only to past acts of force, fraud, aggression, and interference.[70]

One response might be to argue that showing property could have arisen justly is all that is necessary. As long as current property holders are not criminals and any relevant provisos are fulfilled, it is up to anyone who would dispossess a current property owner not only to show that theft or fraud exist in the history of property, but also to show the person making the claim is heir to a victim of a specific instance of unjust transfer of property. Such "statute of limitations arguments" (as I call them) have a significant weakness: they can justify governments' ownership of taxation and regulatory powers with as much or more plausibility as they can justify individual ownership of the incidents they hold.[71]

Another response to the claim of irrelevance might be to rely on metaphorical appropriation: people who find profitable market niches have, in a sense, appropriated their gains through labor mixing or other

[66] Widerquist, *Lockean Property Theories*.

[67] Tully.

[68] Simmons, 303–304; Sreenivasan, 103–104, 112–117.

[69] Macpherson, 211–213; Waldron, *The Right*, Chapter 6.

[70] Mautner, Thomas (1982). "Locke on Original Appropriation." *American Philosophical Quarterly* 19: 267–269, m 267, 286.

[71] Widerquist, 2009.

criteria. Versions of this argument have been put forward by many property rights advocates,[72] but they beg the question of why the *system* of property rights in which these actions are taken is justified. Grant S. McCall and I have used extensive anthropological and historical evidence to argue that the private property system was imposed by aggressive, government-sponsored interference with people who fulfilled virtually any suggested appropriation criteria and exercised their freedom (or their rights as appropriators) to establish common access to land. The book also argues that the private property system could not plausibly have come about without such extensive aggression against common people.[73]

The defense of the overall theory against the charge of irrelevance is still underexplored. It seems that whatever theory one uses to justify the gap between the original appropriator and the current property holder becomes the entire theory of modern property rights.

By ignoring this problem, many property rights advocates tacitly rely on special pleading. They claim that government ownership of territory is unjust because past governments established their powers without a just connection to original appropriation, but they also claim that private ownership of land is just even though past private owners established their powers without a just connection to original appropriation.[74]

5 A Menu of Lockean Property Theories

The following outline summarizes the above discussion of the range of Lockean unilateral appropriation theories. Each point leaves the choice of interpretation open to reflect the conflicting conclusions Lockean authors have drawn from this broad body of ideas.

5.1 *Outline 1: A Broad Outline of Lockean Theories of Property*

(1) In a state of nature, individuals have equal claim, or equal lack of claim, to unused natural resources (particularly land), meaning that resources are [one of the following]

[72] Kirzner, *Discovery*, 98–100; Lomasky, 130; Nozick, 158–161.

[73] Widerquist and McCall, *Prehistoric Myths*.

[74] Widerquist "Dilemma"; Widerquist and McCall, *Prehistoric Myths*; Widerquist and McCall, *The Prehistory of Private Property*.

(A) unowned, or
(B) owned in common, for the use of everyone but the property of no one, or
(C) collectively owned as if by a corporation in which everyone owns a share.

(2) In the state of nature, a natural resource may be unilaterally appropriated, [all three of the following]

(A) by the first person(s) [one or more of the following]
(i) to alter it significantly through work,
(ii) to use,
(iii) claim,
(iv) possess, or
(v) discover it,
(B) because [any combination of the following]
(i) people have an unconditional right to use resources to secure their needs (and wants?) without interference;
(ii) the first laborer deserves the benefit of their efforts;
(iii) the modified asset embodies the appropriator's labor;
(iv) labor improves and accounts for most of a good's value;
(v) improving land effectively makes more resources available for others;
(vi) property can help overcome the tragedy of the commons;
(vii) a stable property rights system creates benefits for everyone; and/or
(viii) property takes a pivotal role in a person's life;
(ix) finders' keepers: only the firstcomer has an unconditional right to use a resource;
(C) providing [any combination or none of the following]
(i) none (no part) of the resource is wasted (*the no-waste proviso*),
(ii) everyone has access to subsistence (*the charity proviso*), and/or
(iii) a sufficient amount is left for others to use (*the enough and as good proviso*).

(3) The (combined) proviso(s) can be fulfilled [all of the following]

(A) either [one of the following]
(i) in kind: in the same resources taken by the appropriator, or

(ii) by replacement, through
(a) market opportunities,
(b) government services, or
(c) cash;
(B) in terms of [either]
(i) standard of living or
(ii) independent functioning, and
(C) at the following level [one of the following]
(i) weak,
(ii) strong,
(iii) extra-strong or,
(iv) maximum strength.

(4) Civil society is established, at which time [both of the following]

(A) property rights [one of the following]
(i) become partially or entirely subject to (and contingent upon) social agreement, or
(ii) are carried over into civil society, because [all of the following]
(a) the propertyless tacitly agree to unequal property,
(b) the protection of property is the reason civil society exists, and
(c) a statute of limitations protects current property holders from the responsibility for past injustices;
(B) the proviso(s) [one of the following]
(i) are partially or entirely obviated by agreement,
(ii) remain in effect but are fulfilled by an unregulated market, or
(iii) remain in effect and justify government regulation of property.

(5) In civil society, the government may not arbitrarily seize property. It may tax and regulate property, [one of the following]

(A) only with the consent of the majority of the governed [any combination of the following]
(i) to protect self-ownership and property rights,
(ii) to maintain necessary government expenditure (such as public roads and services), and/or
(iii) to enforce whatever provisos remain in effect (if necessary); or

(B) only with the individual consent of each specific owner.

Which specification of the outline best reflects Locke's original intent is beside the point, because as I've said, Locke's intent might be unknowable, and it is not necessarily the most valuable or logically strongest theory that can be extracted from the line of reasoning he pioneered.

One could pick and choose almost anything on this outline to create a theory with some textual claim to be Lockean. Perhaps Lockeanism's malleability helps maintain its popularity.

A focus either on unilateral appropriation with no need for validation through agreement or on a general agreement to create property without unilateral appropriation might be stronger than Locke's hybrid. A streamlined argument for unilateral appropriation would focus on the method and justification of appropriation (point 2), and justify property in civil society with some statute of limitations (4:A:ii:c) without relying on tacit agreement. The main areas of controversy are the appropriation criterion(s) (2:B), the provisos (2:C and 3:C), whether government action is necessary to fulfill the provisos (4:B:ii–iii), and the corresponding strength of property rights (5).

The interpretations and reformulations of Lockean theory mentioned above can be characterized largely as specifications of this outline. For example, Nozick[75] greatly streamlines Lockean theory to justify strong property rights. His most important premises are his unspecified theory of acquisition (2) and the weak proviso (2:C:iii and 3:C:i):

5.2 *Outline 2: Nozick's Property Theory in Terms of the Lockean Outline*

(1) In a state of nature, individuals have an equal lack of claim to unused resources. Meaning that natural resources are

(A) unowned.

(2) In the state of nature, some unspecified theory justifies appropriation,

(C) providing

[75] Nozick.

(iii) a sufficient amount is left for others (*the enough and as good proviso*).

(3) This proviso can be fulfilled

(A) in the following form:
(ii) by replacement, through
(a) market opportunities
(B) in terms of
(i) standard of living,
(C) at the following level:
(i) weak.

(4) Civil society is established, at which time,

(A) property rights
(ii) are carried over into civil society, because
(c) a statute of limitations (partially) protects current property holders;
(B) the proviso
(ii) remains in effect but is fulfilled by an unregulated market.

(5) In civil society, the government may not arbitrarily seize property. It may tax and regulate property,

(A) only with the consent of the majority of the governed
(i) only to protect self-ownership and property rights

There may be a tradeoff between the strength of the theory and the strength of the property rights it supports. If an appropriation supporter accepts more limits, they can make the argument for appropriation more widely acceptable, but they may make the property rights they are able to justify less valuable to holders. Supporters of strong private property rights have two kinds of options. They can argue against the need for limits on appropriation,[76] or they can accept limits, and argue that strong private property rights do not violate those limits.[77]

Opponents of appropriation and strong property rights need to be aware of all of these strategies and be ready to address the entire menu of options available to supporters. There are at least four ways to do so. First, they could take issue with the statute of limitations (4:A:ii:c). This strategy

[76] Kirzner, *Discovery*; Narveson, *The Libertarian Idea*; Rothbard.

[77] Mack, "The Self-Ownership Proviso"; Nozick.

would not refute the idea of appropriation in the abstract, but it could possibly refute its practical relevance. Second, they could argue that the provisos (3:A–C) are necessary and cannot be fulfilled within the context of conventional property rights. Third, they could argue that none of the eight reasons for appropriation (points 2:B:i–viii) justify putting non-appropriators under the duty to respect property rights. Fourth, they could argue, as McCall and I have, that the application of these principles in our world's history has not, and likely could not support the kind of highly unequal private property system Locke and right-libertarians invented appropriation theory to rationalize.[78]

The ambiguity that Locke allowed to creep into his property theory has developed into a diverse set of appropriation-based justifications for private property that must be fully addressed by opponents.

[78] Widerquist and McCall, *The Prehistory of Private Property*.

CHAPTER 4

Lockean Appropriation Assessed

The great aim of the struggle for liberty has been equality before the law.
—F. A. Hayek[1]

Let me make this point before I meander: what's good for the goose is good for the gander.
—Webb Wilder[2]

This chapter criticizes the Lockean theories of unilateral appropriation outlined in this chapter, evaluating their case for appropriation against the standard of providing maximal equal freedom for all. This chapter showed that appropriation under the maximum-strength version of the Lockean proviso (resource abundance) is consistent with equal freedom for all, and this chapter assesses whether any of the components of Lockean property theory (the reasons for appropriation, the strong-version of the proviso, and tacit agreement) can extend unilaterally appropriated property beyond the state of resource abundance. I will follow the points of "Outline 1" from the previous, addressing the most powerful versions of the main points on the outline one by one, concluding that these points, individually or in concert, fail to establish that unilateral appropriation of full liberal ownership rights (or any strong property rights) is consistent

[1] Hayek, *The Constitution of Liberty*, 85.

[2] Wilder, W. (1989). "Hittin' Where It Hurts." Island Records.

K. Widerquist, *The Problem of Property*, Exploring the Basic Income Guarantee, https://doi.org/10.1007/978-3-031-21948-1_4

with maximal equal freedom. That is, Lockean property theory fails to make strong property rights more than legal privileges.

1 Unilateral Appropriation Diminishes Joint Claims Out of Existence

If people begin with strong collective property rights, either there can be no private property rights or private property is contingent upon social agreement. The important point in any such argument is the justification of the strength and form of initial collective ownership or nonownership. If natural resources are initially unowned, it does not necessarily follow that they are up for grabs. Anyone who argues that unowned resources are up for grabs must explain why resources are unowned and why nonownership entails resources being up for grabs rather than unownable. One strategy is to concede the opposing premise, to argue that private ownership can be derived from common resource ownership or that common ownership can be derived from unowned resources.

Locke attempts to derive private appropriation from a common claim to resources, but he does so by defining common ownership claims so narrowly as to make them practically nonexistent. He states that everyone has equal claim to the Earth (premise 1:B), but individuals get only two things for their common claim to ownership of the Earth: the right to appropriate unowned resources (in the unlikely event they find any) and the proviso. Even if resources are initially unowned, the reason most people don't have the opportunity to appropriate is that laws protect existing owners.

How can this problem be reconciled with maximal equal freedom? This question does not rely on a claim to collective ownership. It relies only on the observation that if resources are unowned, they are *equally* unowned by everyone. To make unequal ownership of initially unowned resources consistent with maximal equal freedom requires at least one of two arguments: either the appropriators have provided a service to others sufficient to earn their property, or they have left enough so that they have done no harm. Therefore, the weight of collective claims is shifted to the method of appropriation and the proviso (point 2:A,B,&C), and none of the arguments put forward here relies on collective ownership of property.

2 Appropriation Based on First Labor (or First Use) Has No Value Without Historical Accuracy

If the historical link to the original appropriator is lost, original appropriation theory implies nothing at all about the distribution of property. The problem is not simply that fails to justify the existing property-rights regime but that it neither justifies changing it nor leaving it the same nor any specific regime. It is simply irrelevant.

A central point of any unilateral appropriation theory is that ownership goes only to the *first* person (or group) who labors with (or uses) a piece of property (premise 2:A). Therefore, all current property rights require a historical link between the current owner and original appropriator. If the resource has been traded, all of the wealth (money) that was traded for it must also be traced back to just original appropriations—not only the money that purchased it in the most recent transaction but all money used to purchase it every time it has exchanged hands since the resource was appropriated. Given that Locke's appropriation theory relies so heavily on historical accuracy, Locke offers a very poor account of how property actually came into existence. McCall and I have presented extensive evidence to show that Hobbes's hypothesis that property begins with the arbitrary decision of the sovereign is much more realistic, as are accounts by Rousseau and Marx in which people aggressively assumed control of resources, sometimes after long conflicts.[3]

A very small amount of land rights in the world can be traced back to the first person to mix their labor with the land. In Western Europe, most ownership rights to land can be traced back to the feudal period when the people who worked the land were distinctly separated from and subordinated to landlords who claimed ownership by force and not by any connection with original labor. In Eastern Europe, many property rights can be traced back to an enormous grab during the fall of communism. The United States is one of the few countries that, for a time, had a policy of granting ownership of land to the first person to farm it. The Homestead Act of 1862 granted 160 acres of federally owned land to the first person who built a house on it and farmed it for five years. Only about

[3] Hobbes, T. (1962). *Leviathan*. Glasgow: Collins, 186; Rousseau, 109; Marx, K. (1994). *Selected Writings*. Indianapolis: Hackett Publishing Company Inc., 294–297; Widerquist and McCall, *The Prehistory of Private Property*.

10% of U.S. land ownership can trace its origin back to such appropriations; not everyone had equal rights to take advantage of the program; and in most cases that land had already been used by Native Americans, many of whom met Locke's labor mixing criterion for appropriation. The few cases of direct connections to the very first users are places that were inaccessible before modern technology, such as the Falkland Islands (and many such places were fought over as well).

Right-libertarians argue that if land were appropriated in a just process, it would have a similar ownership pattern to the one we see today. I first argue that claims what would have happened cannot justify unequal rights. At the very end of this section, I argue that the claims about what would have happened are false.

That is hardly a justification. Suppose you are arbitrarily arrested. The police explain, "every time there is a crime, we imprison someone. The same *pattern* of inequality of rights exists in our country as in countries with 'due process of law.' Therefore, you have nothing to complain about." The argument that justice would involve putting someone in prison is not a justification for simply putting anyone in prison. Arrest interferes with you, and saying that there might be a justifiable reason for one person to interfere with another in this manner hardly justifies their arbitrary interference with you.

Property owners could conceivably defend their holdings if they could argue, "We are the legitimate successors to people who did something to entitle themselves to it." But they cannot defend their holdings by arguing, "If there were people who did something to entitle themselves to this property, and if their legitimate successors were identified, they would have the same privileges over someone that we claim over you."

If the theory of original appropriation is not a myth, metaphor, hyperbole, or propaganda, world society is under a strong obligation either to make a few Native Americans very, very wealthy.

An insistence on property by individual appropriation based rather than on some replacement theory would demand that certain people, who cannot possibly be identified, are entitled to large holdings. Such a theory is not relevant to the world we live in. For almost all property on Earth, the link to the first appropriator is lost forever. Someone out there is the legitimate successor of the original appropriation of every piece of property. If original appropriation theory is correct, it implies that whatever we do with property today will be an injustice to the heirs of the anonymous appropriators.

Be that as it may, we need a theory of what to do when the original appropriator cannot be found, but that is not original appropriation theory. That is a replacement theory, and it has a very different starting point. Even if original appropriation theory is morally correct, it is irrelevant to the way property is or should be distributed in the world today. The replacement theory of what to do when the connection is lost becomes the *only* relevant theory for virtually all property. Locke, Nozick, and Jan Narveson do not specify this theory and dwell instead on a fiction.[4]

Original appropriation theory is a distraction from this other unspecified replacement theory that would be capable either of justifying current property rights or of indicating how property rights must be changed to become just. Nozick mentions an unspecified principle of rectification, but the name implies that it is a theory of returning property to the true successor of the original appropriator.[5]

The replacement theory is not simply a matter of returning property to the true owner, but finding another way to begin a line of property when there is no way to find the true successor of the original appropriator. This theory, whatever it is, must become the *entire* theory of property. If unilateral appropriation theory is irreplicable, no one can claim ownership, aside from the legitimate successors of the original appropriators. Therefore, it will be difficult for an unspecified replacement theory to explain why some people have more claim than others to the ownership of external assets.

One might argue in response that the burden of proof ought to rest on those who would interfere with the current property holder, but there are two problems with this reasoning: first, the burden of proof is usually invoked in cases of punishment, when one is in a position with fewer rights than others or when one's rights are being reduced. But it is the property owners who have assumed greater privilege than the propertyless and reduced the rights of the propertyless, implying that the burden should be in the other direction. Further, it is those who argue against redistributive taxation who argue for changing people's rights status. For generations, governments have claimed the right of taxation for any purpose that suited the sovereign, including many purposes far less noble

[4] Locke; Nozick; Narveson, *The Libertarian Idea*.

[5] Nozick.

than support of the indigent. Prohibition of redistributive taxation and the establishment of a right-libertarian minimal state would be a major change in property rights and a significant decrease in the rights status of the propertyless.

Second, there is no lack of proof—it is a historical fact that current ownership rights did not emerge from a series of legitimate transactions going back to the original appropriators. This is not a minor problem; unilateral appropriation theory rests on the premise that everyone has equal claim (or equally lacks claim) except for the original appropriator. If the current holders do not have that link, they have no more claim to the resources they hold than everyone else. If we take seriously the right-libertarian claim that the justness of the current situation depends entirely on the justness of the events that brought it about, all property must have had a just origin to be legitimate. If, instead, all past violations are forgiven and their advantages now protected, the obvious strategy is to lie, cheat, and steal today, and argue for recognition of past property rights tomorrow. The attempt to justify property on fiction is not an argument for rights but for legal privileges.

The claim that the highly unequal ownership system would have developed anyway is not only logically irrelevant, but it also happens to be empirically false. In, *the Prehistory of Private Property*, McCall and I use extensive historical evidence to show that appropriation theory does not favor individual rights to private property. Anyone who could reasonably be identified as an "original appropriator" almost anywhere in the world established common or complex, flexible, overlapping, and at least partial common and collective property systems. The private property system was established by a long campaign of aggressive, violent interference of privileged people against common people who overwhelmingly used their freedom to appropriate shared access to common land. The ownership system so familiar today could not plausibly have developed from that starting point by any means other than violent, aggressive interference.[6]

[6] Widerquist and McCall, *The Prehistory of Private Property*.

3 Original Appropriation as Metaphor

If the appropriation story says nothing about how the private property system came into existence, what is the value of this appropriation-based theory that has been at the center of the debate for three centuries? Perhaps it has metaphorical value: every owner does something equivalent to appropriation. The story of original appropriation might represent the idea that people who have worked to get ahead under the existing rules should be allowed to stay ahead. If metaphorical appropriation works, it functions as the missing replacement theory for a literal original appropriation theory. In the metaphor, the state of nature represents the previous generation of property owners and appropriation by labor mixing represents trading one's labor with them to become an owner. Every trader metaphorically appropriates property. My trade with the previous generation of property holders makes you no worse off than before. Anyone of us can make trades with property holders, and in that sense, all the property of the world is available for appropriation.

A problem with this metaphor is that equality before the current generation of property holders is not the same as equality before the law or equality before nature. Property owners are legally endowed with the right to distribute property according to their whim. They don't have to accord equal right to metaphorically appropriate property to anyone, and so people begin in a state of inequality. Property law creates the situation in which everyone in one generation is born equally eligible to attempt to satisfy the whims of the previous generation of property owners. Therefore, property in the metaphorical appropriation story is a legal privilege.

Another problem with the metaphorical appropriation story is that it seems either to beg the question or to regress to the literal story of original appropriation. If I succeed in trading my labor for property and you are left propertyless, you are no worse off than *at the start*: you are still propertyless. But your propertylessness *at the start* is what the story is meant to justify. Why does the current generation of property holders get to decide who is and is not privileged in the next generation? Because the previous generation of property holders gave them that power. Why did the previous generation of property holders have that power? Because the generation before... and on and on until you get to the original individual appropriator, who is a fiction.

If the metaphorical story can justify property at all, the act of appropriation through trade has to do something for the propertyless. Current property owners have to show that their reason for approach (2:B) and/or the proviso imposed on appropriation (2:C) somehow promote maximal equal freedom. Therefore, the attention next turns to point 2:B in the outline.

4 What Is Labor Supposed to Do in Appropriation Theory?

This chapter argued that if the maximum-strength proviso holds (resource abundance), nothing else is necessary to justify the unilateral appropriation of property. Whether I add value to a piece of property by laboring with it or whether I simply take it does not matter as long as there is more than enough to go around. What, then, is the role of labor?

Labor can give one reason why a person might claim a particular piece of property, but it is not necessarily decisive. Suppose Gilligan labors with a previously untouched piece of land when abundant land of the same value in every sense is available for everyone. Any attempt to take that land from Gilligan is apparently nothing more than an attempt to take the fruits of his labor. Labor works in that case, but suppose Gilligan and Mary Ann both have a claim to the same piece of land. Gilligan's claim is based on labor mixing, and Mary Ann's claim is based on a sentimental attachment—her grandmother died on that spot. Neither claim is inherently more consistent with maximal equal freedom, and a decision in such a dispute might reasonably go to the person with the longest-standing claim rather than the person with the labor-claim.

One could argue that people who labor more deserve more than people who do not, but that is not a freedom-based claim, and I am only considering freedom-based claims. If the maximum-strength proviso is fulfilled, certainly there is greater equal freedom if anyone can appropriate natural resources for any reason rather than restricted reasons. Therefore, the labor mixing argument (2:B:ii) does not establish the greater right to property than other kinds of claims. This sort of reasoning, I believe, partly explains why many modern right-libertarians have replaced the first labor with other criteria.[7]

[7] Nozick; Narveson, *The Libertarian Idea*.

If the labor criterion is important, labor or some analogous attribute of ownership is needed to give the metaphorical appropriation story any weight. Some attribute of labor, such as value added, has to make up for the inability to fulfill the maximum-strength proviso.

5 Labor Does Not Fulfill the Proviso If It Is Not Otherwise Fulfilled

According to Locke, labor accounts for most of the value of property (premise 2:B:iv), and this improvement effectively makes more resources available for others (premise 2:B:v). Perhaps laboring to improve land is meant to compensate people for taking it out of a collective in which there are not enough and as good resources left in common for others. Sreenivasan argues that because laboring so greatly increases the output of land, it satisfies the proviso almost necessarily.[8] However, Cohen argues that, in terms of *noninterference*, this argument can only be true when a large commons' exists and the population is small enough that every time someone appropriates property the ratio of the size of the commons to the number of people who live on the commons increases.[9] The compensation-based argument is one of increased opportunity rather than increased freedom from interference.

Sreenivasan's contention is not necessarily true in an economy with scarce land without some limit on property that forces the benefits of increased productivity to be shared with the propertyless. A person, who appropriates full liberal ownership rights improves the resource for their own benefit, but they are under no obligation to share the value of improvements with the propertyless. Suppose Mr. Howell takes some land that produces a given amount of coconuts without cultivation, and improves it so that it produces ten times what it produced before. The appropriator has the *ability* to give the propertyless the fruits of the land he could have gotten if it were left in common, but as the owner of the land *and* the improvements he makes to the land, Mr. Howell is at liberty to keep all of its fruits or to charge Gilligan the full value of his improvements *plus* the full value of the land, which could make Gilligan worse off than he was in the state of nature.

[8] Sreenivasan, 57.

[9] Cohen, 187–188.

Unless appropriators are forced to pay some kind of rent or tax on the resources they hold, there is no mechanism that puts them under an obligation to share the value of their improvements with people without property. If Mr. Howell wants Gilligan to work, he needs to pay him no more than it takes to motivate a starving person to work for survival, and if he doesn't want Gilligan to work for him, he doesn't necessarily have any reason to share the benefits of production with Gilligan at all.[10]

Even if the appropriator offers a wage that converts effort into consumption at a greater rate than a person could do with access to commonly held property, there are two reasons why it is not the same as taking nothing at all. First, the appropriator blocks others from making the same or a similar appropriation.[11] Appropriators have the opportunity to capture the benefits of trading not only their labor but also the property they work with. Wage laborers have no such opportunity. Gilligan might be as well off as he would be with access to land in common, but not as well off as he would be if he could appropriate land and trade it as Mr. Howell does. The privilege to take free resources and to be paid both for one's improvements to them and for the resources themselves is one that cannot be granted to everyone under a system of unilateral appropriation and full liberal ownership.

Second, appropriators offer wages in exchange for service, which, because of the power relations it entails, may not be as valuable as the ability to work for oneself, even if it affords a higher standard of living.[12] Suppose Gilligan likes to walk in the woods and gather coconuts. But just as he is about to do it, Mrs. Howell appropriates the land, saying, "No problem. You can be my butler. You can bring me my coffee, make my bed, and draw my bath. I will make sure that you spend fewer hours per day working and receive more coconuts than you would, if you gathered them yourself on common land." Mrs. Howell has offered Gilligan a higher standard of living, but Gilligan might have reason to think it is not enough and as good. Any theory of *unilateral* appropriation specifically rules out asking the propertyless whether their new options are enough to fulfill the proviso.

[10] Competition between employers will not ensure the proviso is fulfilled. A supply of workers who need a job to survive might keep wages at levels that make the net benefit of work less than the net benefit of being one's own master in Locke's state of nature.

[11] Otsuka.

[12] Cohen, 79–80.

If laboring with resources does not compensate others for the loss of resources, what function does it perform? If non appropriators are not entitled to a share in the improvements of land created by the labor of the appropriator, it makes no difference to them whether the appropriator labored to improve it, labored to make it worse, or did not labor with it at all. Unless some part of the value of improvements is put toward compensation for those who have less, distributing natural resources according to labor seems to be a needless restriction on freedom and a legal privilege for those who attained property. However, holding owners to that obligation is a departure from full liberal ownership, and if the level and form of compensation must be negotiated, property rights depart entirely from unilateral appropriation.

6 The Size of Labor's Contribution Cannot Give One Group Exclusive Claim to All the Land

Perhaps the statement that labor improves the value of resources (premise 2:B:iv) is meant to show that the value of natural resources is so small that it is completely irrelevant. Locke asserts that labor accounts for the greatest portion, perhaps 99/100ths, of the value of property. This statement appears to imply the argument that people who demand redistribution based on a claim to natural resources are actually attempting to acquire value created by labor.

Locke's claim about the value of natural resources is questionable, and his argument for it is fallacious.[13] Locke credits human effort with 99% of the value of output because a farm produces more than 100 times more food than one could gather on uncultivated land. If he applied the same factor-attribution method to natural resources, he would have to credit natural resources with 100% of the value of output, because labor produces no food at all unless it is mixed with natural resources. Using Locke's factor-attribution method, the two factors together account for 199% of the value of output.

Even if there were some objective way to measure the "value" of inputs, even if it were true that labor accounted for most of the value of improved land, and even if the current owners were entitled to all of the value added by all people who have labored with property in the past,

[13] Cohen, 182–185.

it would not give the propertied class claim to *all* the land. These factors provide no reason to ignore the proviso in kind or in something of equal value for those who are blocked from appropriation by others' ownership of scarce resources. The value added by previous laborers does not explain why individuals who would like to acquire scarce assets and improve them should be denied that opportunity by others who asserted no more than that same right.

No matter how large the contribution of labor is to the value of assets, making all access to natural resources contingent upon service to the ownership class makes access to natural resources a legal privilege and inconsistent with maximal equal freedom for all. Suppose the previous generation took possession of everything, improved its value 100-fold, and designated a small group of people in the current generation to have complete control over those resources. The improved value of property does not change the fact that property rights interfere with people who might like to take raw resources and increase their value by their own effort.

The argument from improvement fails to eliminate the privileged aspect of property. If access to resources is inconsequential to the propertyless, why is it so consequential for the heirs and designees of past owners? As Waldron argues, it is impossible to argue from the standpoint of equal rights for a special right that is only legally available to some.[14] One cannot say, from the standpoint of equal rights, "You should respect my property for I would respect yours if you had any."[15] If the right to appropriate property is consequential for people who manage to appropriate something, it cannot be inconsequential for those who are legally blocked from appropriation by the appropriated property rights of others. Such a system of appropriation cannot establish property as something other than a legal privilege.

[14] Waldron, *The Right*, 423–445.

[15] Ibid., 441.

7 Appropriation Conflicts with the Right to Unconditional Subsistence on Which It Is Based

One plank in Locke's justification of appropriation is the "paradox of plenty:" People would starve despite the abundance available in nature if they had to wait for unanimous approval before they could use resources. Doing so, he relies on an unconditional right to subsistence or to the resources necessary to produce subsistence (2:B:i),[16] and even a right of access to the resources to produce for one's wants as well.[17] But unilateral appropriation does not secure an unconditional right to subsistence for everyone—only for the appropriators. Unless ownership rights are weakened, unilateral appropriation blocks access to an unconditional right to subsistence for the propertyless. The comedown from a broad-based right to subsistence (2:B:i) to the finders' keepers ethic (2:B:ix) is inconsistent with equal freedom.

The connection between an unconditional right to subsistence (2:B:i) and a right of unilateral appropriation of property (2:A) is not true. The most expensive goods don't need to be privately held to ensure survival. I need private control of the food I eat and the cotton I wear, but those items can be grown on public, common, or rented land. Subsistence can be secured through collective projects or by private access to common, collective, or unowned resources.

The paradox of plenty is cooked to make common ownership look bad by proposing a unanimous consent rule for any decisions about common resources. Anthropologists have documented thousands of peoples who view the land as common property. None of them use a unanimous consent rule, and none of them have had a problem with a paradox of plenty preventing them from maintaining subsistence.[18]

If the "paradox of plenty" has any value, it is not in the coordination problem of agreement but in the need for *unconditionality*: people ought to have the right to take the resources required to produce the goods they need for survival without anyone else's consent. It is not true that

[16] Locke, §28.

[17] Locke, §31.

[18] Widerquist and McCall, *Prehistoric Myths*; Widerquist and McCall, *The Prehistory of Private Property*.

people who live on common lands actually starve for want of consent, but it is plausible to say that no one's permission ought to come between an individual and the means of their preservation. If no one has more claim to resources than anyone else, and if human life is valuable, unconditional subsistence is essential to any meaningful conception of maximal equal freedom.[19] The meaningful principle behind the "paradox of plenty" is that *everyone has the same unconditional right to use natural resources to meet their needs* and perhaps their wants as well.

One could argue that there are mechanisms in Lockean property theory—such as the right of charity and the enough and as good proviso—to ensure that people have a right to subsistence and perhaps even a right to thrive. Property owners have a responsibility to make sure there are enough jobs available to secure employment and subsistence for everyone. There is no bargaining power on either side: workers have the responsibility to work and property owners the responsibility to employ them. They cannot impose involuntary unemployment on propertyless workers.

The problem with this argument is that employment lacks the *unconditionality* that appropriators enjoyed and that is where the privilege lies. The most generous full employment policy imaginable cannot mean that employees can do whatever work they want without the consent of their employer. The right to work without anyone else's consent is not the right to a job, but the right to direct, unconditional access to resources. If it is objectionable for society to place conditions between appropriators and their subsistence even though appropriators have *some way* of attaining subsistence, then it is also objectionable for society (or employers) to place conditions between propertyless workers and their subsistence even though workers have *some way* of attaining subsistence.

Unilateral appropriation (without compensation for the propertyless) puts the propertyless worker in the same position as the constrained appropriator in Locke's paradox of plenty: in need of someone else's consent to attain the resources they need for survival despite the plenty of resources available. It is no better—and possibly worse—to be prevented from attaining the means of subsistence by having to ask permission of a property-owning class than by having to ask permission of a collective body representing society. There are no known historical cases in which

[19] And ECSO freedom: Widerquist, *Independence*.

people starved for want of unanimous consent to access common land,[20] but people do die of complications of economic deprivation (such as malnutrition, exposure, and disease) because they are unable or unwilling to meet the conditions that governments and employers put between them and survival.

The propertyless are worse off than they would be even under the strawman of unanimous consent. Under unanimous consent, everyone must strike a deal with them to survive: as long as no one is suicidal, everyone lives. But under capitalism, propertied individuals have no need to strike a deal with all of the propertyless to survive[21]: if capitalists are uninterested in what you are able to do for them, you die and they barely notice.

The argument behind the "paradox of plenty" simply cannot support the division of property into haves and have-nots. If *unconditional* access to the means to support oneself is a right and not a privilege of property owners, a right to employment is not enough for the propertyless; they need some form of *unconditional* compensation either in cash or in resources. If we are concerned about the paradox of plenty, we must be concerned about it for the propertyless as well. Without unconditional access to resources or unconditional compensation, property rights make the unconditional right to survive not a universal right but a legal privilege for the ownership class.

8 Locke's Consent Theory Lacks Consent

None of the arguments for unilateral appropriation have succeeded in establishing exclusive property rights to scarce external assets. The remaining tool in the Lockean kit is implied consent based on the acceptance of money (premise 4:A:ii:a), but it is a very weak argument.

The mere valuation of money hardly represents consent to a specific property-rights regime. Homeless people value money, but they hold neither land nor currency. I do not see the logical connection between the mere fact that they would like to have money (but don't) and their consent to others' appropriation of all the land that they would also like to

[20] Widerquist and McCall, *Prehistoric Myths*; Widerquist and McCall, *The Prehistory of Private Property*.

[21] Cohen, 96, 100–101.

have (but don't). The primary reason they want money is that it can buy the things they could get from external assets—a place to sleep, food to eat, etc. Their desire for money cannot be taken as evidence for anything more than a desire for the means to get the resource access the monetary economy has deprived them of.

This kind of "consent" theory could justify extremely oppressive relations. Suppose a slave works all year for his master. On New Year's Day, the master gives the slave a few pennies to buy liquor to celebrate. If the slave accepts the money, Locke's argument implausibly implies the slave has therefore consented to the property-rights regime that made them property. It would be outrageous to say they are no longer a slave but a willing worker. The slave did not have a choice in bringing the system about, and he would not accept the pennies if refusing them would bring about another system. Many people who would find it in their interest to trade their valuation of money for a share of national wealth. Waldron argues that those who are least well off in a monetary economy are those who are least likely to have had a say in bringing the monetary system about, and that consent to putting a value on money is not the same as consenting to inequality.[22]

Any argument justifying capitalist inequality on tacit consent uses an unreasonably generous definition of "tacit." If someone picks up my book, looks me in the eye, motions toward the door, and then walks out with my book, I have tacitly given my consent to take it. It is clear because I could easily have stopped them. Propertyless people have no similar opportunity to object. If they want to live, they cannot say, "I refuse to participate in the monetary economy because I do not consent to the property-rights regime." A person might be willing to consent to something that they are forced to do, but the fact that they do it under force is no evidence of their consent.[23] As Carole Pateman writes, "Unless refusal of consent is possible, talk of consent is pointless."[24]

Perhaps Locke means that a monetary economy is good for people, even though it entails inequality. He could say that people do or would consent to a monetary economy as opposed to the alternative, and therefore they consent to its inequality. However, there are many different

[22] Waldron, *The Right*, 224–225.

[23] Otsuka; Widerquist, *Independence*, 158–162.

[24] Pateman, C. *The Disorder of Woman*. Cambridge: Polity, 12.

kinds of monetary economies with different levels of inequality and with different people in positions of authority; and little or no evidence that propertyless people are better off in the one that makes them destitute. Early modern philosophers made a similar argument for the rule of kings.[25] Therefore, everything you own is attributable to the protection of the king. Without a government to protect you, all of your property would be stolen. John C. Calhoun made a similar argument to justify slavery.[26] Now that we know that chaos is not the only alternative to absolute monarchy, and poverty is not the only alternative to a property system that creates propertylessness,[27] The consent argument has no value in supporting those institutions.

Many people often do voice complaints about the prevailing property-rights regime. To say that none of these complaints are valid or that no complaints can possibly be valid is to lose a legitimate claim to a consent-based theory.

If consent is the right strategy for justifying property, it has to be genuine consent. If complaints are valid and consent is necessary to legitimize a property-rights regime, unilateral appropriation is illegitimate.

9 What Kind of Ownership?

Locke lists a few limits to ownership, but he confers full or nearly full ownership[28] to the family of the appropriator. Many subsequent scholars have explicitly employed Lockean theory to argue for full liberal ownership. But little connection to the strong rights of full liberal ownership is given in, or discernible from, Locke's unilateral appropriation theory. Locke's arguments for labor mixing and value added by labor seem to imply ownership to no more than the value added by labor, and the unconditional right of access to resources establishes no more than use rights, not ownership.[29] As argued above, the "paradox of plenty" and the equal right to use natural resources to satisfy individual needs and

25 Hobbes.

26 Calhoun, John C. (1851). "Disquisition on Government." *Constitution.org*. http://www.constitution.org/jcc/disq_gov.htm.

27 Widerquist and McCall, *Prehistoric Myths*.

28 In the sense of Honoré's 11 incidents, see above.

29 Waldron, *The Right*, 161–162.

wants imply powerful limits on property rights to assure every generation has the same right of equal access to resources.

Locke seems to believe that the end of government is to protect property rights,[30] but that a specific definition of property rights exists prior to and with greater authority than government or any agreement among individuals. Who decided that full ownership is what property must be, and why are the propertyless bound by that person's conception of what property should be? This institution can't be consistent with consent and maximal equal freedom unless the propertyless agree to the incidents of ownership. A weaker version of property rights could be made consistent with consent or compensation for the propertyless or with some version of an equal right to appropriate for all.

To reject Lockean appropriation, I need to address its most appealing aspect, which Simmons describes as, "those who … usefully employ some unowned good ought to be allowed to keep it (if in so doing they harm no others)."[31] This idea is appealing, if it holds. The problem is that when it fails to hold, it is difficult to see where the harm comes from. The harm is not in any one owner's action but in the system. Owners benefit from a system that defines rights so strongly to exclude most people from becoming owners, and privileges people who manage to do so.

If I work hard and honestly, and acquire property, I have personally hurt no one and benefited all of the people I have traded with, but I have benefited from a system that hurts someone. It is easy for me to lose sight of the fact that the people I have benefited are the previous owners of property, not the people who have to make do with fewer resources because I have more. If I pass a homeless person on the street, I have access to more land than he does and more gold, more jet fuel, more clean water, more oil, more wood, and more of every resource the world has to offer, and I thereby force him to take less of every resource. What have I done *for him* in exchange for my larger share? Nothing.

A unilateral property-rights regime is not wrong because people who work hard sometimes get ahead; it is wrong because people can only get ahead by working for the wrong people. The system is set up so that the only people I need to serve to gain access to a larger-than-minimal share of natural resources are those who previously controlled larger shares of

[30] Ibid., 161–162.

[31] Simmons, 223.

resources, and the government will interfere with everyone else to force them to accept my share. When did they agree to accept this burden—what free agreement does this follow from? None. Lockean theory cannot show that this follows from any sense of equal freedom or rights. The system neither follows from nor preserves liberty.

The metaphorical interpretation of the appropriation story embodied in Simmons's quote does no more than distract our attention away from the system and toward the actions of individuals within it. That strategy might have great rhetorical value in defending the system, but it has no logical value in justifying the system.[32]

Chapter 5 considers whether modern right-libertarian formulation of unilateral appropriation theory can do any better.

[32] I don't accuse Simmons of endorsing this strategy. He merely recognizes its appeal.

CHAPTER 5

Right-Libertarian Appropriation Assessed

> The very beginning of Genesis tells us that God created man in order to give him dominion over fish and fowl and all creatures. Of course, Genesis was written by a man, not a horse. There is no certainty that God actually did grant man dominion over other creatures. What seems more likely, in fact, is that man invented God to sanctify the dominion he had usurped for himself over the cow and the horse.
>
> —Milan Kundera, *The Unbearable Lightness of Being*[1]

Modern right-libertarians tend to use a stripped-down version of Lockean unilateral appropriation in which first labor is replaced by first use or first claim, and the proviso is deemphasized. For simplicity, this chapter uses Nozick and Narveson as spokespersons for the two most common right-libertarian treatments of the Lockean proviso: using it but arguing that it has virtually no policy implications or arguing that the appropriation principle needs no proviso at all. I could have used many other right-libertarians as spokespersons for these two views. I refer to other right-libertarians as I go, and I address a wider range of libertarian thought in several other works.[2]

[1] Kundera, M. (1999). *The Unbearable Lightness of Being*. London: HarperCollins.

[2] Widerquist, "Libertarianism;" Widerquist, "Dilemma;" Widerquist, *Independence*; Widerquist and McCall, *Prehistory Myths*; and Widerquist and McCall, *The Prehistory of Private Property*.

K. Widerquist, *The Problem of Property*, Exploring the Basic Income Guarantee, https://doi.org/10.1007/978-3-031-21948-1_5

Both Nozick and Narveson base their reasoning on some concept of not harming. Nozick argues that some weak proviso is necessary to ensure everyone is as well off as before appropriation. Narveson argues no proviso is necessary because no one has any positive right in anything until it is appropriated, and so there is no question of harm. Another right-libertarian, Israel Kirzner, dismisses the proviso on the grounds that the value the appropriator takes does not exist until they discover and thereby create it.[3]

This chapter argues that these authors must define harm so narrowly that substantial reductions in freedom do not count as harm. But by doing so, they are unable to make an argument that establishes property consistently with maximal equal freedom, and their arguments are unable to limit government in the way they would like.

Section 1 discusses Nozick's weak version of the proviso. Section 2 discusses Narveson's proviso-free appropriation theory. Section 3 shows that the principles these authors establish, consistently applied, cannot limit government to a minimal state but could actually justify an extremely strong state, such as a for-profit monarchy. Section 4 criticizes right-libertarianism as an after-the-fact justification that cannot be consistently applied from inception without contrary-to-fact historical assertions. Sections 5 and 6 place these arguments in context.

1 The Weak Version of the Proviso

Nozick's property theory usefully clarifies differences between end-state distribution theory and entitlement theory, but as a defense of right-libertarian entitlements, it fails largely because the crucial argument is missing. Nozick seems to take the institution of full liberal ownership for granted and simply does not offer an argument why property rights must necessarily be so strong.[4] Nozick simply ignores losses of liberty and privileges created by strong property rights.

Nozick drops some of the less appealing points of Locke's theory, such as the connection between first labor and appropriation (opting for first

[3] Nozick; Narveson, *The Libertarian Idea*; J. Narveson (1998). "Libertarianism vs. Marxism: Reflections on G. A. Cohen's *Self-Ownership, Freedom and Equality*." *The Journal of Ethics* 2 (1); and Kirzner, "Entrepreneurship, Entitlement, and Economic Justice."

[4] C. C. Ryan.

use). He concedes that a historically based theory of first appropriation requires a genuine connection to the first appropriator, and although he argues that such a measure would only be necessary in the short run, he goes so far as to say that something like Rawls's difference principle could be used as a rough rule to rectify past injustices. After all past injustices have been rectified, no further redistribution will take place; any pattern of ownership that is consistent with the weak proviso is just.[5]

He makes the metaphorical appropriation story somewhat more explicit. His Henry Ford example is meant to show that the effects of an initial set of holdings wash out over time and eventually become irrelevant. "If anyone would have bought a car from Henry Ford, the supposition that it was an arbitrary matter who held the money then ... would not place Henry Ford's earnings under a cloud."[6] If society were to begin trading from a position in which every individual supported themselves, then great inequalities would appear.[7] Wouldn't the just distribution of property be whatever followed from voluntary trade or "capitalist acts between consenting adults?"[8] If the distribution of property is merely the expression of the voluntary interaction of individuals, then why should any particular pattern be more just than another?

Nozick's discussion of what rights are in general and where they come from is brief,[9] and he has been roundly criticized for this omission.[10] For the right to appropriate, he spends several pages critically discussing Locke's theory of appropriation without being entirely clear whether he is endorsing it or building his own theory.[11] Nozick simply concludes, "I assume that any adequate theory of justice in acquisition [appropriation] will contain a proviso similar to the weaker of the ones we have attributed

[5] Nozick, 231.

[6] Ibid., 158.

[7] Ibid., 184.

[8] Ibid., 163.

[9] Ibid., 9–10, Chapter 3.

[10] Nagel, Thomas (1983). "Libertarianism Without Foundations." In *Reading Nozick: Essays on Anarchy, State, and Utopia*, Jeffrey Paul (ed.). Oxford: Basil Blackwell, 191–205; Sheffler, S. (1981). "Natural Rights, Equality, and the Minimal State." In *Reading Nozick: Essays on Anarchy, State, and Utopia*, J. Paul (ed.). Oxford: Basil Blackwell, 148–168; and Fried, B. H. (2005). "Begging the Question with Style: Anarchy, State, and Utopia at Thirty Years." *Social Philosophy & Policy* 22 (1): 221–254.

[11] Cohen, 74.

to Locke,"[12] and "I believe that the free operation of a market system will not actually run afoul of the Lockean proviso."[13]

Although Nozick's explanation can be ambiguous,[14] as I understand it, he essentially pares down the theory of appropriation to the weak version of the Lockean proviso. That is, metaphorical appropriators may take whatever property they want, for whatever purpose, as long as everyone else is no worse off than if *no one* had appropriated *any* property and all resources were still unowned.[15] In the sense that workers have a higher living standard than hunter-gatherers in a hypothetical state of nature, a society with a property-owning class and a propertyless class can be consistent with the proviso.

Nozick's argument may have some force against the belief that realizing a particular pattern is all there is to distributive justice, but that's a false dichotomy. Nozick's argument fails as a defense against the argument that full liberal ownership does not promote maximal equal freedom as well as other unpatterned property-rights systems. The parts of Nozick's argument that he dwells on are largely true, but they only function to distract from the harms that unilateral appropriation inflicts on the propertyless and from the lack of justification in his theory explaining why property must be defined as full liberal ownership.

1.1 The Argument Ignores or Begs a Central Question

Why must property rights be so strong? Nozick's essay is presented as an answer to that question, but he never actually addresses it. Consider his Henry Ford example again, which is supposed to show that the effects of the arbitrary aspects of the initial set of property holdings wash out over time as property goes to its most productive members.[16] To the extent that trade washes out the initial set of holdings, it does so only if readers take the institution of full liberal ownership, or some other strong set of property rights, as given. The implied argument is: full liberal ownership

[12] Nozick, 178.

[13] Ibid., 182.

[14] Wolff, J. (1991). *Robert Nozick: Property, Justice and the Minimal State*. Cambridge: Polity.

[15] Nozick, 178–179.

[16] Ibid., 158.

exists. Someone like Henry Ford improves the production process for automobiles, increasing the value of existing property, and thereby, accumulates a large amount of property. Assuming purely voluntary trade (no fraud, externalities, etc.), Ford's actions do not harm anyone else, relative to their position immediately before trade. Anyone without property is no worse off than they were before Ford began trading. Therefore, any restriction on Ford's property rights punishes someone who has harmed no one. Therefore, strong property rights must continue to exist.

The problem with this argument is that the strong property rights that the example is supposed to justify exist at the outset.[17] Henry Ford does not harm the propertyless, because the institution that made them propertyless existed before he came along. It is not the trade of property rights, but the existence of strong property rights that causes propertylessness. As long as private property includes the absence of terms, transmissibility, and so forth (see Chapter 4), people will be born without property. Henry Ford's attainment of those property rights by trade, given the existence of the institution of full individual ownership, is inconsequential.

The Wilt Chamberlain example does very much the same for future trades. Nozick stresses that the example begins with a given pattern of property holdings in place (whatever pattern the readers believes is just), but he doesn't call attention to the fact that the example also begins with the institution of full liberal ownership in place. Under that institution, people willingly trade their property for the service of watching Chamberlain play basketball, making him rich and everyone else a little poorer.[18] Thus, all the perils of propertylessness and poverty are supposed to flow from voluntary exchange.

However, at least for anyone who is born later, voluntary trade had nothing to do with it. Assuming there is no propertylessness in the initial pattern, it comes into existence because one generation established the institution of full liberal ownership and thereby assumed the right to decide who does and does not have access to resources in the next generation. Propertylessness follows from the existence of the institution of full liberal ownership that exists unquestioningly at the beginning and the end of both examples. Nozick gives no argument why the property that

[17] That is, it begs the question. Dworkin makes a similar argument and reply as a hypothetical without connecting it to Nozick: Dworkin, R. (2000). *Sovereign Virtue: The Theory and Practice of Equality*. Cambridge, MA: Harvard University Press, 88.

[18] Nozick, 160–164.

people trade is defined so strongly, and therefore, these examples cannot function as a defense of that institution. It merely gives the impression of a dichotomy (full liberal ownership or patterned principle of justice) that happens to be false. If Ford and Chamberlain traded under an institution with weaker property rights, their trades would not need to be accompanied by the propertylessness of others.

1.2 The Weak Proviso Ignores Significant Harms

Right-libertarians might argue for a weak version of the Lockean proviso on the basis that it leaves non-appropriators no worse off and no better off than they were before appropriation, in the sense that they have access to living standards that are as high as they would have if they were hunter-gatherers in a state of nature. They are entitled to remain unharmed by others' appropriation, but they are not entitled to share in the benefits of others' appropriation.

This reasoning ignores the many things natural resources do for people other than helping them reach a certain consumption level. As Chapter 4 argued, people have an interest in appropriating resources individually, appropriating them collectively, or using them without ownership, and all of these possibilities are prevented by the strong property rights of others, but none of those uses count for Nozick's weak proviso. As Cohen asks, "Why should institutionally primitive common ownership be the only alternative?".[19]

By establishing the institution of full liberal ownership, the legal system interferes with (and therefore, reduces the negative freedom of) anyone who would like to live under a different system. In any case, to say that appropriation benefits the appropriators and leaves the propertyless no worse off than they were before is not sufficient to say that it extends equal liberty. The appropriators take legal rights to natural resources that are defined in a way that precludes others from taking the very same rights. Property still opposes the equal liberty to use natural resources and remains, therefore, not a special right but a legal privilege. The institution makes them worse off by interfering with what they might have chosen to do, even if they are better off than the worst alternative defenders of the system can imagine.

[19] Cohen, 87.

1.3 The Weak Proviso Violates the Principle of Justice in Transfer

Why should there be *any* proviso at all? To admit that appropriation requires even a weak proviso admits that the appropriation of natural resources interferes with propertyless people's ability to use common resources, thereby depriving the propertyless of the liberties they would otherwise have. Nozick's principle of justice in transfer, applied consistently, would require respect for people's liberty to use common resources unless they voluntarily agreed to give up that liberty.[20] Appropriators take away these liberties without consulting the people who lose them and give them something else instead. Allan Gibbard argues that the strict libertarian position would be that the propertyless could only give up whatever claim they have to common resources by consent.[21] As long as Nozick recognizes *any* claim to unowned resources, his principle of justice in original acquisition conflicts with the principle of justice in transfer.

Avoiding this issue, Nozick's argument becomes suddenly paternalistic.[22] He argues for coercing people in a state of nature to make them propertyless proletarians, who are initially (i.e., before trade) much worse off than people with direct access to common resources. But by granting extensive property rights to others, this coercion reaches an end-state distribution, justified by giving them positive opportunities, which, he supposes, will make them better off.

This argument is not merely similar to—*it is the same* as the argument that if the government may take money from you to build an opera house, you will be better off after you use the opera house or interact with people who have been enriched by the opera.[23] Nozick normally decries that kind of argument as a violation of justice in transfer. He claims to believe that rights are inviolable; and that "the state may not use its coercive apparatus for the purpose of getting some citizens to aid others, or ... for their *own* good or protection."[24] Nozick fails to defend freedom from coercion for the propertyless as he does for the rich; he is not arguing for rights but for privileges.

[20] Nozick, 150.

[21] Gibbard, A. (2000). "Natural Property Rights." In *Left-Libertarianism and Its Critics*, Peter Vallentyne and Hillel Steiner (eds.) Basingstoke: Palgrave, 23–30, 25.

[22] Cohen, 89–90.

[23] Widerquist, *Independence*, 125–129.

[24] Nozick, ix.

1.4 *Nozick's Proviso Gives Workers Nothing for Their Claim to the Land*

In any property system, there must be some contingency for compensation for involuntary transfer. Suppose I accidentally destroy your house. You can sue me for the market value of your house, but you cannot sue for how much you would have charged me if I had asked for permission beforehand, even if you really would have sold only for several times its market value. Compensation might include a penalty premium, but some form of compensation has to fill the function of rectifying an involuntary transfer.

That much supports the proviso, except, as this section argues, Nozick's version doesn't actually offer any compensation. He writes, "Compensation would be due those persons, if any, for whom the process of civilization was a *net loss*, for whom the benefits of civilization did not counterbalance being deprived of these particular liberties."[25] The benefits of civilization he recognizes include wages that do double duty, compensating people for work performed and for the coercion necessary to put them in the position where they had to work for wages—all for one low price.

To see this, consider two groups of propertyless workers. Imagine that one group of workers has a claim to natural resources and the other has none. Imagine two scenarios. (1) Advantaged people buy the resources from the workers who have a claim to them for \$X, which is enough to satisfy the weak proviso. Then they offer jobs at a wage of \$Y to both groups. The group with a claim ends up with \$X + \$Y. The group with no such claim gets \$Y.

(2) Advantaged people appropriate the natural resources and offer jobs to all of the workers at the same market wage of \$Y, which happens to be high enough to satisfy the weak proviso. The workers with claim to resources receive the same as the workers without claim. It's only logical for the workers to complain, "My wages are for my labor, what have I received in compensation for my claim to resources?" The answer is nothing: access to property under unilateral appropriation is the privilege of the proprietor, and the weak, post-trade proviso effectively reduces any resource claim to nothing. The weak, post-trade proviso inherently

[25] Ibid., 178f.

recognizes a claim to resources, and then effectively discards it. Perhaps the weak proviso should be discarded instead.

2 Resources as Unowned

Narveson discards the proviso altogether, arguing that people have no claim to the Earth: "*none of it* belongs to *anyone, individually or collectively.*"[26] Many writers, including both supporters and opponents of unilateral appropriation, have assumed that if assets are unowned, they must naturally be up for grabs,[27] but there is a missing connection in that supposition. The sea, atmosphere, and rivers are unowned but not up for grabs. Who says which resources are up for grabs and which aren't? Land, like the air and the sea, could be treated as a commons: both unowned and incapable of being owned. Many cultures known to history and anthropology treated some or all of their land as a commons.[28] If one wants to argue that unowned resources are naturally up for grabs, then one needs to give some reason why unowned things must be up for grabs rather than simply unownable. Reliance on an unargued assumption that it's just natural is a non-argument, no better than, "Because I say so." Self-ownership does not make the connection. It is possible to protect self-ownership without establishing property in external assets.[29]

Narveson uses a rather odd application of the principle of noninterference to explain why unowned resources are up for grabs. The first person to claim a resource owns it because "second-comers would then be *interfering* with the courses of action initiated and being continued by those first-comers."[30] He argues that there is no more to property than this, presenting his theory as a derivation of unilateral appropriation from the consistent application of the principle of freedom as noninterference. But, to do this, he has to answer the question of whether the first comer's appropriation interferes with anyone else who might want to appropriate

[26] Narveson, "Libertarianism vs. Marxism," 10, emphasis original.

[27] Nozick; Cohen, 84, 114–115.

[28] Widerquist and McCall, *Prehistoric Myths*; Widerquist and McCall, *The Prehistory of Private Property*.

[29] Widerquist and McCall, *Prehistoric Myths*.

[30] Narveson, "Libertarianism vs. Marxism," 11.

resources or might already be using those resources without appropriating them.

Narveson's argument that appropriation does not interfere with the propertyless relies on a distinction between interference and prevention. According to Narveson, if you stop a person from doing something after they start (or perhaps after they formed the intentioned of starting), you interfere with them, but if you stop people from doing something before they start, you merely prevent them. By establishing property, the appropriator merely *prevents* others from doing things they had no previous plans of doing; he does not *interfere* with their doing anything they had already planned to do. Therefore, he concludes that appropriators do not need to bother with any proviso. They may take whatever they want to use even if that prevents another person from being anything more than a "starveling."[31]

The next two subsections discuss two critical problems with Narveson's distinction between prevention and interference.

2.1 Equal Freedom from Prevention

Narveson fails to apply his theory of freedom from prevention consistently. If it is not important that the propertyless are prevented from appropriating property, neither is it important that the propertied class is prevented from appropriating property or from appropriating with full liberal ownership rights. What Narveson actually wants—freedom from prevention for the wealthy but not for the poor—is not a right but a privilege.

The government's prerogative to tax and regulate property was well established long before any entrepreneur alive today was born, and long before the concept of entrepreneurship or a market economy existed. Therefore, under a consistent application of Narveson's theory, government prerogative does not *interfere* with current property owners at all; it merely *prevented* owners from assuming strong property rights and it began preventing them before they ever attained the notion of being property owners at all.

The interference-prevention distinction eliminates the right-libertarian argument against taxation, at least as far as current property owners are

[31] Ibid., 23.

concerned. If governments' power to tax and regulate property interfered with anyone, it is those long-dead individuals who happened to own property when governments first declared their power to tax. In North America, of course, any such people would have been Native Americans, most of whom treated all or most of their land as a commons. The claims of current property holders all stem from titles given to them by governments that had already established the power to tax before seizing resources from Native Americans.[32]

Narveson is using the strawman of thinking collective ownership with something like a unanimity rule is the only alternative to privatized land, when in fact, most stateless people treat land as a commons where unownable land is freely accessible to everyone, and no one needs anyone's permission to hunt, gather, fish, farm, or scavenge.

The concept of a commons is more than a theoretical problem for Narveson's attempt to eliminate the proviso by appealing to a distinction between prevention and interference because excellent evidence shows that indigenous peoples used almost all of the world as a commons long before a campaign of government-sponsored aggression forced privatization on an unwilling world.[33] By Narveson's own distinction, the people who established the commons were the firstcomers, whose rights, had they been respected, would have *prevented* privatization long before it began, but they would not have *interfered* with anyone. Also, by Narveson's distinction, the long aggressive colonial campaign that leads to privatization of the Earth should be viewed as unethical *interference.*

2.2 No Ethical Distinction Between Prevention and Interference

Narveson has a consistency problem not only in the application of the prevention-interference distinction but also in his attempt to show that it reflects some deeper principle of respect for individual self-governance. He repeats Locke's inconsistency on an unconditional right to appropriate centuries later. Arguing for the rights of the first comer to assume ownership, Narveson says they do not have liberty without an unconditional right to property, "Since a very large part of the point of having a right is precisely that you *do not* have to get anybody else's permission, that is a

[32] Widerquist and McCall, *The Prehistory of Private Property.*

[33] Ibid.

fatal objection to any thought that universal common ownership exemplifies *liberty*."[34] Ten pages later he denies that anyone else needs this right, "That the starveling is so badly off that he will not last long if he does not accept a proffered job, or whatever, is not the fault of those who offer it, nor, quite possibly, of anyone."[35]

If the unconditional right to appropriate property is something essential to the freedom of primordial appropriators, then it is also essential to the freedom of contemporary "starvelings." If it is not important to the freedom of starvelings, neither can it be important for appropriators. If it is acceptable for the propertied class to prevent the propertyless from appropriating resources, it is equally as acceptable for the government to prevent the propertied class from appropriating full liberal ownership rights. One cannot have different standards of freedom for the rich and the poor and have any claim to support equal liberty for all. If the lack of unconditionality is fatal to collective ownership's claim to exemplify liberty, it is also a fatal objection to any claim that appropriation and full ownership rights exemplify liberty. Therefore, Narveson's theory is not one of rights and freedom but of legal privileges at the expense of freedom.

If there is value in the concept of freedom as noninterference, it must mean freedom from all constraints imposed by others, not merely freedom from *new* constraints. Suppose, as I am being born in a vacant lot, someone builds high walls around it, effectively imprisoning me. At the time of my birth, I had no current plans to leave the lot, and as Narveson argues, I have no natural right to the land outside the lot. Therefore, the continued maintenance of the walls, the building of spikes on the walls, and the posting of guards on the walls, all to prevent me from climbing out, do not "interfere" with me; they merely "prevent" me, and under Narveson's theory, as stated, they are not ethically troubling in any way. Only if the people who imprison me wait until after I attempt to leave the lot before they begin their efforts to keep me in, do they "interfere" with me. For Narveson, there is supposed to be some important moral difference between the two, but he does not say what it is.

[34] Narveson, "Libertarianism vs. Marxism," 13, emphasis original.

[35] Ibid., 23.

According to Narveson, the contention that appropriation interferes with the propertyless implies people have a positive right in things,[36] but it says nothing at all about a right in things. It says only that preventing people from doing things involves interfering with them. The question I am examining here is not what are "natural property rights," but what set of property rights confers the maximal equal freedom from interference. The firstcomer rule greatly frees the first comer from interference, but only by allowing firstcomers—with the help of the legal authority's enforcement power—to interfere with all the secondcomers. A freedom-based theory has to derive its rights from freedom, not the freedoms it allows from its theory of rights, and certainly not from a circularity, such as freedom is having these rights because having these rights is what it means to be free.

3 State Appropriation of Property[37]

Right-libertarians typically advocate unlimited inequality of wealth and see this as parallel to advocating limited government.[38] Nozick, for example, argues that the justness of distribution is entirely determined by how it came about rather than by any principle evaluating the pattern of the end-state distribution.[39] But these authors don't examine the full implications of having *no restrictions* on inequality. This section argues that any theory of unlimited wealth has to allow monarchy, at least in the sense in which one person owns all the property in a given area, and assumes through that property right nearly all of the powers of a government authority. Therefore, virtually unlimited government power is consistent with right-libertarian property theory.

This section shows how monarchy can grow without violating Nozick's principles of justice in acquisition and transfer, and without violating the principles of other right-libertarians. This exercise will show two things: first, that right-libertarian principles, consistently applied, do not necessarily lead to a limited government and, second, that right-libertarian

[36] Ibid., 11.

[37] This section was later expanded into the article: Widerquist, "Dilemma."

[38] Narveson, *The Libertarian Idea*; Narveson, "Libertarianism vs. Marxism;" Nozick; Kirzner, "Entrepreneurship."

[39] Nozick, 150–160.

principles allow a property-owning class to assume powers over propertyless individuals that right-libertarians would not allow a state to assume over entrepreneurs.

Anarchy, State, and Utopia tells a fanciful story in which the development of the state begins after natural resources have been appropriated into private property through unilateral appropriation (reversing the actual time-line by thousands of years).[40] Nozick examines how a state could develop out of mutual-protection associations, but that is not the only fanciful story one could tell. Suppose all the land on an island called "Britain" is appropriated by a relatively small portion of the population following whatever rule of appropriation right-libertarians prefer. All proprietors prefer to protect their property themselves, and they are not interested in joining mutual-protection associations. Propertyless people come to proprietors seeking land, materials, and protection in exchange for labor, money, or obligation to help the proprietor protect her estate and the people who live or work there. Suppose each proprietor insists that any propertyless people who wish to live on her estate must accept her as the arbiter of all disputes. Individuals may band together to protect their nominal self-ownership from the proprietor, but all disputes involving property are the sole domain of the proprietor.

The proprietor creates different sorts of deals with different people. To some, she sells permanent tenancy rights, a sort of quasi-ownership called a "title" that tenants can buy and sell from each other so long as they recognize that the proprietor retains lordship over all property. She thereby retains rights to charge a royalty on all titles, to reclaim any rights granted under the title at any time, and to change the royalty rate or the conditions under which a person holds a title.

Other tenants might live on the proprietor's land without quasi-ownership of it. The proprietor may allow them to rent from quasi-owners with the understanding that she has the right to collect rent directly from them in whatever form she wants or indirectly through the holders of titles. She can take a portion of their income, a portion of their sales, a portion of their work-day in work directly for her, etc. This trade is voluntary in the sense that it follows the principles of "justice" in appropriation and transfer. As the owner, she sets the terms for anyone who wants to

[40] Widerquist and McCall, *The Prehistory of Private Property*.

spend any time at all on her estate. Anyone who doesn't like it is welcome to negotiate a deal with another proprietor.

The proprietors find it advantageous to form strategic marriage alliances and to use the custom of primogeniture in inheritance. Proprietors defend themselves from aggressors and sometimes seize the land of aggressors in accordance with Nozick's rectification principle. Over the generations, land holdings get larger as marriages, inheritance, and rectification join estates together, until one day one proprietor owns the entire island of Britain and decides to call herself "Queen" rather than "proprietor," and she prefers to call her holdings her "realm" rather than "estate." But the nature of her proprietorship has not changed. She owns and manages it as she wishes with no interference from big government. She now prefers to refer to her "tenants" as "subjects," her "royalties" as "taxes." But the nature of these payments hasn't changed. They are voluntary transfers that fulfill all of Narveson's and Nozick's criteria for justly acquired property. It doesn't matter what the Queen does with her tax revenue. She can use it for her own amusement, for public works, for the common defense, or for alms (call it "redistribution") to the poor. Her revenue is her profit on the titles she allows her subjects to hold. It is, therefore, her property to do with as she will.

After several generations, the quasi-landowners begin to forget that the Queen is the heir of the original appropriators of land, and begin to think that they had somehow appropriated the land, and should have full liberal ownership rather than the quasi-ownership the Queen allows. They could espouse right-libertarian theory as a justification for their complaints against the Queen's taxation and regulation, but it would be an attempt at usurpation. It would amount to saying that through just acquisition and transfer we have attained the level of holdings X (our current level of ownership subject to the Queen's taxes and regulations), and we, therefore, are entitled to the level of holdings X+ (our current level of ownership plus freedom from the Queen's "interference"). They are looking at themselves as just appropriators of the land, who have unjustly been denied full rights of that ownership, but they have forgotten that they only hold such titles as the Queen has established, and she has always retained the right to tax and regulate.

Consider the Queen a "property-owning monarch" to reflect the "just" (according to right-libertarian principles) method by which she came to power and the minor limits on her power that we can derive from right-libertarian principles. What restrictions are there on such a monarch? Nozick's and Narveson's principles imply that the Queen has to respect the nominal self-ownership of her subjects, and Nozick adds that the Queen has to respect the weak proviso. It is possible that a parliament could develop to protect citizens' rights—such as they are—against the Queen. Individuals cannot use parliament to protect "property rights" because they don't have any. The Queen can't order a person beheaded, but under Narveson's no proviso provision, she could order them to be deprived of food and water. Nozick's weak proviso would disallow that, but she would have no responsibility to allow anyone to attain a living standard higher than they could in a state of nature. A confiscatory tax above that point would be within the Queen's rights.

The parliament could pass laws about how people could treat each other, but the Queen would have the power to decide whether to allow any of her property to be used to enforce these laws. They can declare war, and she can decide whether any property will be used for war. Effectively, she has nearly all the power of an ordinary monarch. The Queen's government is just in terms of right-libertarianism because it does everything a right-libertarian minimal state is supposed to do: she protects everyone's nominal self-ownership, and she protects the property rights of everyone who happens to own property—i.e., herself.

JPA gives two reasons to believe that the Queen's subjects are profoundly unfree. First, her subjects have no ECSO freedom.[41] Their status as free, self-owning individuals is purely nominal. They must provide service for the Queen to get access to the resources with which they can produce any of the necessities of life. Second, the Queen has privileged property rights that violate the principle of maximal equal liberty. She was born with privileges of ownership that block them from assuming any of the same privileges.

Unfortunately for right-libertarians, the Queen's subjects are unfree in the same way that propertyless people are unfree in right-libertarian society. To see this, simply re-read the above story substituting "property-owning class" for "Queen." Therefore, right-libertarians are unable to object to the Queen on the above grounds. The story of the property-owning monarch presents a dilemma for so-called property-rights advocates.[42] They can accept that a property-owning monarchy is

[41] Widerquist, *Independence*.

[42] Widerquist, "Dilemma."

consistent with right-libertarian freedom and lose their claim to principled support for minimal government, or they can reject the property-owning monarchy and lose consistent advocacy for full liberal ownership of property.

If right-libertarians take the first option, they would have to admit that right-libertarianism is not classical liberalism, but a form of royalist conservatism. They have created an argument for property rights so strong that it cannot function as an argument for *private* property rights. However, state-ownership of property isn't limited to monarchy. If a Queen can be the successor to the appropriators of property, so can a democratic community. The Queen could choose to bequeath ownership of her realm to a democratic community, or it would be easy to retell the appropriation story replacing the Queen with a democratic cooperative.[43]

If right-libertarians take the second option, they will find it impossible to apply any argument against the state-ownership of property that does not also apply to a capitalist class. Consider three such attempts.

3.1 This Story Is Not Literally True

Although this story is not literally true, this is probably the worst reason a right-libertarian could propose to defend private title holders, because the story of the private Lockean original appropriation is not literally true either.[44] The propertied class is not actually the successor of the original appropriators, nor did the people who have any reasonable claim to be original appropriators actually choose to establish anything like a right-libertarian private property system.[45]

The only appropriation story that has any hope of holding up without original individual appropriation is Kirzner's metaphorical version,[46] but this story, which gives property to whoever has the more senior claim, supports the Queen. Every piece of property in Britain traces back to a title granted at the monarch's pleasure. The Queen is the heir of a title that was established nearly 1000 years ago. The title-holding landlords and landladies of Britain were later granted titles by the British monarchy.

[43] Ibid.

[44] Ibid. Widerquist and McCall, *The Prehistory of Private Property*.

[45] Widerquist and McCall, *The Prehistory of Private Property*.

[46] Kirzner, *Discovery*; Kirzner, "Entrepreneurship."

Even the names "title" and "landlord" reflect the royalist origin of private property. The Queen has transferred much of her property rights to parliament, but she and her ministers have never relinquished the power to take, regulate, and redistribute property.

All of the property rights to 40% of the world's surface stem from treaties signed by agents of the monarchs of England. It is hard to find any private property titles in the world that cannot be traced back to "the arbitrary distribution of [some] sovereign"[47] somewhere. One might think of Native American Reservations, but those are owned by tribal *collectives* rather than capitalist individuals. Therefore, the unilateral appropriation story points to the government or the people collectively, rather than the capitalist class, as the ultimate landlord.[48]

3.2 Taxation Is Forced Labor

Consider Nozick's argument that taxation is on par with forced labor,[49] writing, "These principles involve a shift from the classical liberals' notion of self-ownership to a notion of (partial) property rights in *other* people."[50] Samuel Wheeler explicitly connects this argument with taxes on property, "No significant moral difference in kind exists between eliminating my ability to play softball by taking my knees away and eliminating my ability to play the market by taking my money away."[51]

It is a mistake to consider the dispute about taxation as having something to do with self-ownership; it is a dispute about property ownership.[52] If you have a valid ownership claim to property, and the Queen takes some of it away, she has violated your property ownership. However, if the Queen has a valid property right in all of the external assets in her realm, her "royalties" or her "taxes" violate neither property rights nor self-ownership. They are simply the expression of her ownership rights.

[47] To borrow a phrase from Hobbes, 186.

[48] Widerquist, "Dilemma."

[49] Nozick, 169–172.

[50] Ibid., 172.

[51] Wheeler, S. (2000). "Natural Property Rights as Body Rights." In *Left-Libertarianism and Its Critics: The Contemporary Debate*, Peter Vallentyne and Hillel Steiner (eds.). New York: Palgrave.

[52] Otsuka.

The Queen can limit people's ability to play the market, not by taking "their" money away but just by taking some of her money back. She even put her picture on the money to remind people that they hold it at her pleasure. If so-called "libertarians" attempt to take away the Queen's ability "to play the market" by collecting taxes on the use of *her* money, they have attempted—in Wheeler's terms—the moral equivalent of eliminating her ability to play softball by taking her knees away.

The supposed effect of taxes on *self*-ownership is actually an effect of taxes on *property* ownership. The Queen's power stems entirely from her control of property; all her subjects maintain full, nominal self-ownership. Her subjects' propertylessness forces them to serve her by paying her taxes, but as Narveson says, this "is not the fault of those who offer it, nor, quite possibly, of anyone."[53] If it is permissible to put the working class in the position where they must give some of their labor to the ownership class to get access to property, then it is permissible to put the title-holding class in the position in which they must serve a property-owning monarch to get access to property. What's good for the goose is good for the gander.

3.3 Queen Has Too Large a Concentration of Power

One might argue that a monarch who owns all resources has too large a concentration of power. That argument requires an end-state, patterned principle of justice, strictly ruled out by Nozick's entitlement theory. The only end-state principle he allows is the weak proviso,[54] which gives the Queen's subjects the right to compare their standard of living to what they would have in the state of nature. Narveson's theory does not even allow them to make that comparison.

The argument that a government monopoly on property is too great a concentration of power falls into the same category as egalitarian arguments against a world in which the richest X% of people own Y% of the world's property. Right-libertarian theories have not typically responded to those arguments by saying that this pattern of distributional inequality is within acceptable limits, but by saying that *any* argument based on a

[53] Narveson, "Libertarianism vs. Marxism," 23.

[54] Cohen, Chapter 3.

pattern of distributional inequality is unacceptable.[55] If they are serious about making an unpatterned argument, they must say that a pattern in which one entity owns all property is also acceptable.

Once a property-owning monarch is shown to be one end-state distribution that could follow from original appropriation as plausibly (or as implausibly) as private ownership, right-libertarianism's call for minarchy or anarcho-capitalism is exposed to be simply a preference for one pattern of end-state distribution over others. The contention that taxation is theft or forced labor relies on the tacit assumption that a pattern of ownership in which the government or the people as a whole have property rights in all natural resources is an unacceptable pattern, but in which a property-owning aristocracy controls all natural resources is an acceptable pattern. Right-libertarians cannot derive this pattern from any more basic principle, because the freedom people lose to the property-owning monarch is the same as the freedom propertyless people lose to a property-owning aristocracy. If the Queen's pervasive ownership is a threat to the self-ownership of the title-holding class, the pervasive ownership of the title-holding class is a threat to the self-ownership of the propertyless.

Kirzner argues that the person who first appropriates the only watering-hole in the desert is entitled to it because he is the first to discover its true value; others could have done the same had they been as alert as the original entrepreneur.[56] On the same grounds, a new-coming entrepreneur cannot complain if an earlier entrepreneur (the government) has previously appropriated the right to *tax* the only watering-hole in the desert. In other words, if a group of people organized as institutions called businesses can appropriate resources in such a way as to have life-and-death power over individuals, a group of people organized as institutions called governments can appropriate resources in such a way as to have life-and-death power over individuals including individuals who call themselves business owners.

[55] Widerquist, "Dilemma."

[56] Kirzner, "Entrepreneurship," 405–406.

3.4 *Conclusion*

These arguments show that right-libertarianism does not imply a minimal state. It has no principled argument for limited government based on equal freedom for all. Once the underlying end-state principle that the government cannot own property is exposed and dismissed, right-libertarian principles do not make an argument for the market economy or limited government, but for unrestricted government for the material benefit of the people who own the government.

Right-libertarianism is not meant to be a simple assertion that "we don't like government ownership of property;" it is supposed to derive that conclusion from deeper principles. If right-libertarians are serious about original appropriation, transfer, rectification, and the usually unmentioned replacement and/or statute of limitations principles being the only ethical principles of property, they have to be serious about accepting the results, and therefore, consistency demands they accept how their principles endorse an extremely strong government.[57] I doubt many right-libertarians will rejoice at the news that governments aren't actually violating their principles after all. Therefore, I suspect that their principles are merely rationalizations.

4 Equal Rights Under the Law and After-The-Fact Justifications for Property

Property theories based on unilateral appropriation and tacit-yet-binding consent are ethically objectionable because they are after-the-fact justifications. Right-libertarians argue that in the beginning, resources are unowned, and people have an equal right to take them. But that starting point is a fiction. The real starting point for the existing private property system in almost all of the world was a long and violent process of disappropriation now known as colonialism and the enclosure movements.[58] The real starting point for any person is the day they were born. Philosophers come along after-the-fact and invent a fictional starting point to help them justify strengthening some rights, weakening others, and maintaining still others.

[57] Widerquist, "Dilemma."

[58] Widerquist and McCall, *The Prehistory of Private Property*.

If, before-the-fact, everyone is told that resources are up for grabs, and everyone is able to grab them, then we could, in some sense, say that unequal property holdings stem from how people choose to exercise equal freedom. But there was no such day. People today are born into a situation in which everything is already owned, and they do not have the same legal rights to attain property as the appropriators. Access to natural resources and anything made out of natural resources is at the whim of the people who have been awarded the legal privilege of holding property. After-the-fact justifications for preexisting privileges have to rely on fictional "rights" that existed before anyone knew they existed and that no longer exist today.

Waldron argues convincingly that people could not agree before-the-fact and in good faith to appropriation of property without compensation.[59] Imagine our castaways are on a floundering boat, and they can see that they will be washed ashore on an uncharted desert island. Mrs. Howell suggests, "Let's make a rule that all resources on this island are up for grabs for the first taker, so that a few of us will have all of them, and everyone else must serve them to survive." It is ridiculous to believe that people would agree to that rule unless they somehow knew they were good at grabbing property.[60] Yet the crux of right-libertarian theory seems to be that unilateral appropriation is the *only* legitimate method to distribute resources *whether or not* people actually do agree to it or would agree to it. Even if everyone on the boat wanted to use some other method to distribute property or some definition of property other than full liberal ownership, right-libertarians seem to believe they should not be free to do it. This is a very strange position to be taken by people who claim to have some concern with liberty.

It is stranger still when the justification is applied only after-the-fact. It is not the justification of liberty or any kind of a right but of privileges akin to the privileges of kings and feudal lords. If right-libertarians want to argue that property rights arise from equal freedom, they have to point to a time and place where every individual is equally free to appropriate, but no such time or place did or could exist.

Even if appropriation starts from Nozick's hypothetical situation in which everyone lives by their own efforts, it is after-the-fact for anyone

[59] Waldron, *The Right*, 171–183.

[60] Ibid., 276–278.

born into propertylessness later. Many, if not all, of the inequalities that concern egalitarians today are starting point inequalities that do not result from the voluntary choices of the disadvantaged members of a given generation.[61] Steiner and Zelleke argue that property rights based on a right of appropriation in one generation that allows bequests to deny equal rights and equal freedom to individuals in successive generations.[62] This argument can be extended from bequests to any form of cross-generational transfer. The current generation can make no binding decisions about the distribution of property rights for the next generation without making some of them less free than others. There might be a way to justify that interference, but it is nonsensical to claim that it is noninterference.

Suppose, for example, that Nozick, Narveson, Kirzner, Wheeler, Mack, and any other right-libertarians you want to name are on that boat with Gilligan and the others. The ship goes down at night in a terrible storm. They all struggle to swim and finally make it to a beach, where they fall asleep from exhaustion. Thinking ahead, Mrs. Howell sets her waterproof-wristwatch alarm and wakes up Mr. Howell, Gilligan, the Skipper, Ginger, the Professor, and Mary Anne. The seven quickly begin using all of the land in some way. When the right-libertarian theorists wake up, the other castaways inform them, "The entire island has already been appropriated. If you want to step out of this narrow part of the beach (which we have declared by compact to be a public park), you must accept our jobs, at our wages, under our conditions. The only jobs open now are washing dishes at two bucks an hour and working weekends."

How will the right-libertarians reply? "Yes, that is your right...Perfectly legitimate. You were first; we will serve, now and forever. We and our

[61] Scanlon, 110–111.

[62] Steiner, Hillel (1983). "Justice and Entitlement." In *Reading Nozick: Essays on Anarchy, State, and Utopia*, J. Paul (ed.). Oxford: Basil Blackwell, 380–382. Zelleke, A. (2005). "Distributive Justice and the Argument for an Unconditional Basic Income." *Journal of Socio-Economics* 34 (1): 3–15. This argument outflanks the justification for appropriation in Kirzner, I. M. (1981). "Entrepreneurship, Entitlement, and Economic Justice." In *Reading Nozick: Essays on Anarchy, State, and Utopia*, J. Paul (ed.) Oxford: Basil Blackwell, 380–411. Kirzner relies on the assertion that the appropriator was not doing anything that the others "were not free to do." A justification for permanent property rights relying on the existence of equal opportunity is irrelevant across generations and it would seem, in any given generation without perfect equality of opportunity, which seems to include every society in every generation.

descendants will faithfully hope for the day when—through our service—you will voluntarily choose to grant us some ownership of property, but if you never do, that is your prerogative."

Or will they say something more like this? "You can't just make rules that say you can take things that we might want without asking or at least warning us first. If you were going to do that this morning, you should have told us last night."

An after-the-fact justification is so unreasonable that *no one*, who is disadvantaged by it, would or should accept it, when they see it happen up close. As Ronald Dworkin writes, "The brute fact remains that some people have much more than others of what both desire, through no reason connected with choice."[63] That condition is the necessary result of unilateral appropriation, which therefore cannot confer property rights that are more than privileges. Without the consent of, or compensation for, the propertyless, strong property rights oppose maximal equal freedom.

5 What Would Have or Could Have or Actually Did Happen?[64]

If any possibility exists to resolve the dilemma for right-libertarianism discussed in Sect. 4, it is this: propose some kind of temporary redistribution as Nozick suggests, but after that, one-time redistribution compensates everybody who might conceivably be one of the heirs of all past property injustices, then we must have a strong private property system with little or no taxation, regulation, and redistribution of property, because that is what would have developed from original appropriation if we could have gotten from there to here without rights violations.

That claim is the empirical premise in which liberal and right-libertarian arguments for strong private property-rights rest. To put the claim more simply: there is something natural about individualistic private property rights. Or, if people are free to appropriate property, they will

[63] Dworkin, R. (1981). "What Is Equality? Part 2: Equality of Resources." *Philosophy and Public Affairs* 10 (4): 284–345, 329.

[64] This section begins the line of questioning that McCall and I explored in much more depth in our two books: Widerquist and McCall, *Prehistoric Myths*; Widerquist and McCall, *The Prehistory of Private Property*.

appropriate individual, private inheritable property. At least since Locke wrote his property theory, we've been taught that individual ownership develops naturally. That's what people want and will create if they're free from interference. Free people will not create common, collective, or publicly owned property unless some collective entity, such as a despotic government, forces them to do otherwise.

Is this true? Is there something natural about individual private property rights?

McCall and I examine this hypothesis in our book, *the Prehistory of Private Property*. We use extensive textual analysis of property-rights literature to show that private property rights really do need and really do use this empirical premise.[65] We examine the evidence right-libertarians have given to support this hypothesis,[66] and we use extensive evidence from anthropology, archeology, ethnography, and history to show that this premise is false.[67]

In fact, the truth is very much the opposite of the individual appropriation hypothesis: people who can be identified as anything like "original appropriators" virtually anywhere in the world (including Europeans and most settlers of European descent) tend to create property systems that are complex, overlapping, flexible, and at least partly collective with significant common elements. Governments aggressively and forcibly established the private property system around the world during the enclosure movement in European and the colonial movement elsewhere. Given this history, the claim that there is anything natural about the supposed right to unequal private property without compensation to the propertylessness is unsustainable.[68]

6 Forget About Ancient History

Perhaps the most plausible argument for strong private property rights would suggest forgetting about their origin: people who hold property today are largely hardworking people who played by the rules and got ahead, and who do not deserve to be suddenly dispossessed. If in the past,

65 Widerquist and McCall, *The Prehistory of Private Property*, 127–177.

66 Ibid., 178–193.

67 Ibid., 194–268.

68 Ibid.

we have given owners an unrealistic expectation of the property rights we would willingly respect, we might be wrong to suddenly dispossess people who have worked hard under past rules, but must we be forever forced to endure capitalism as the punishment for our sins?[69]

To the extent this argument is valid, it cannot be an argument for full liberal ownership or any strong, permanent property rights; it is Bentham's argument of legitimate expectation, and it justifies no more than a reasonable maintenance of whatever laws are in force.[70] It cannot be used to justify strengthening property rights by making them immune to powers of taxation that all property owners were led to expect long before they started accumulating their property. It can justify a phase-in of changes in taxes, but it cannot justify an argument that society must stick with or strengthen the current property-rights regime no matter its detrimental effects on the freedom of people who own little or no property in external assets.

7 Conclusion

There is no certainty that ancient people were naturally endowed with a positive right to appropriate property that propertyless people lack today but are bound to respect. What seems more likely, in fact, is that propertied people invented the right of appropriation to justify the dominance they had usurped for themselves over property and the propertyless.[71]

Right-libertarians want to apply a principle of voluntary, uncoerced agreement only *after* the establishment of property rights, but they endorse a property-rights system, which can only be established coercively in a way that interferes with the propertyless without any voluntary agreement on their part and which forces them to accept agreements they would not accept without force. Cohen argues that right-libertarians are, in fact, entitlement theorists who put historical entitlements and a narrow conception of self-ownership above a broader conception of liberty.[72] But he does not go far enough. Right-libertarians are not advocates of

[69] This is a reference to Nozick, 231.

[70] Bentham, J. (1931). "Principles of the Civil Code." In *Jeremy Bentham: The Theory of Legislation*, Etienne Dumont, Richard Hildreth, Charles Kay Ogden, and C. K. Ogden (eds.). London: Routledge and Kegan Paul; Waldron, *The Right*, 196–198.

[71] See Kundera.

[72] Cohen, 68–73.

freedom or rights but of legal *privileges*. Full individual ownership puts the privileges of fictional appropriators above any meaningful conception of noninterference, freedom, liberty, self-ownership, equal rights, or voluntary agreement.

To maintain a coherent position, right-libertarians need to admit that they favor privileges in opposition to freedom. It is not a freedom-based argument to say that replacing feudalism with a market economy reduces the liberties of kings, dukes, earls, and lords. Although it does reduce their negative freedom, it does so by reducing privileges they claimed at the expense of equal freedom for commoners. It is not a freedom-based argument to say that replacing Stalinism with democracy reduces Stalin's liberty. In the same way, it is not a freedom-based argument to say that replacing a privileged system of property with a system that defines property by agreement reduces the liberty of privilege holders. Such arguments are not consistent with negative freedom, equal rights, or equal protection of the law.

The attempts to derive a strong, special right to private property from noninterference, self-ownership, or the no-harm principle fail. If scarce natural resources are unowned, they are equally unowned by everyone. There is nothing a person can do unilaterally to establish a property right without denying equal freedom to the propertyless.

In the absence of unilateral appropriation, what rule for privatization of unowned resources is fair? What rule is consistent with maximal equal freedom? It is at this point where the libertarians get it right. "The question, 'when is a deal fair?' ... has only one reasonable answer: when each party is free to say 'no.'"[73] That principle must be consistently applied to the establishment of property and to subsequent trade, not only after pervasive, one-sided property privileges dressed up as "rights" have been established.

A genuine concern with minimizing interference requires the application of the principle of voluntary agreement not only to the *exchange* of property rights but also to the *establishment* and *definition* of property rights. How to do this is the subject of the next chapter.

[73] Narveson, "Libertarianism vs. Marxism," 21.

CHAPTER 6

The Approximation of a Property-Rights Accord

We're all stuck here for a while. Let's try to work it out.

—Rodney King[1]

The previous chapters rejected unilateral appropriation and other justifications for the existing system of strong, individualistic private property without an explicit responsibility for those who own, control, use, or use up more of the world's natural resources and the external assets we make out of them without compensating those who therefore have less access to resources. If people have equal rights and are equally free, and if resources are equally unowned by everyone, how can they become owned by anyone?

This chapter argues for the following method in answer to that question: society approximates a negotiated accord such that people who want to own resources agree on the price and terms of a lease in which they pay for the duties their ownership imposes on others. The justification for a private property involves both the compliance with regulations and the payment of taxes for distribution to those who have less, in the same way that renting property from a private landlord involves paying the price and obeying the terms they set. That is, one person acquires exclusive property rights by compensating others for the duties their ownership imposes

[1] King, Rodney, in his Can't-We-All-Get-Along speech trying to quell the 1992 Los Angeles Riots.

K. Widerquist, *The Problem of Property*, Exploring the Basic Income Guarantee, https://doi.org/10.1007/978-3-031-21948-1_6

on them. I use the term "acquisition" for any method to obtain property other than unilateral appropriation.

Taxation of property, in this theory, is not "interference" with an existing ownership right but a part of the purchase price of the property. Taxation of the right kind is not akin to taking from an established property right, but it is necessary to establish property rights in any external asset. Thus, it is no more interference and it is paid for the same reasons as the private portion of the purchase price of the property. If a unanimous agreement were reached, the compensation could come in almost any form agreeable to the payers and recipients—cash or specific goods and services—but without unanimity, this chapter argues that a substantial portion of redistribution must come in some form of BIG (such as UBI) to give recipients the widest choice of what to do with their compensation.

Section 1 outlines the concept of a property-rights accord in ideal theory in which, by a unanimous agreement, owners pay for the duties they impose on nonowners, and whatever system they agree on establishes property rights that are beneficial to and accepted by both owners and nonowners. Section 2 discusses barriers to achieving the ideal property-rights accord. These include overlapping generations, the improbability of unanimity, and the undesirability of irrevocability. Section 3 discusses how to approximate an accord to create a property rights system in non-ideal circumstances, given the existence of those barriers. This discussion implies both limits on and protections of property rights.

Section 4 considers a possible left-libertarian reply, concluding that although the concerns presented in this chapter are, in a sense, left-libertarian, the argument presented gives reason to reject the most familiar left-libertarian property theory and policy. Section 5 considers a possible right-libertarian reply about why people with resource-intensive lifestyles pay higher taxes. Section 6 summarizes and concludes.

1 A Property-Rights Accord in Ideal Theory

Suppose Gilligan and Mary Anne find themselves stranded alone together on an island in a vast nature reserve. Both recognize that they have equal moral worth; that they have no ownership claim to the island's resources, neither individually nor collectively; and that they should find ways to work together when agreeable and stay out of each other's way as much as possible when working together is disagreeable. There is nothing to stop them from agreeing, for the time being, to dedicate some resources to Gilligan's exclusive use, some to Mary Anne's exclusive use; some for joint projects, some for use by both as a commons, and some for no one's use to partially maintain the environmental function of the nature reserve they live in.

Except for environmental considerations, there is no ethically right mix. There is only the question of what these two want to do. They can by voluntary accord—and without coercion—establish whatever mix of private, public, and common property they want. Any such accord is not quite an ownership agreement; it is an agreement to treat resources they know to be ultimately unowned as if they were property. It holds only as long as Gilligan and Mary Anne continue to agree, and it has no bearing on any other castaway who might appear on the island. But this example establishes the kind of agreement necessary to create something like a property "right."

The observation that there is no right mix is far-reaching. As long as ownership reflects a general accord, it does not need to involve equal division, any particular set of incidents of ownership in privatized resources, or any particular mix of common, collective, and private ownership. Gilligan and Mary Anne can hold all resources jointly or designate almost any portion of resources for exclusive use.[2] Mary Anne can provide services for Gilligan in exchange for a larger share of resources. And there is no natural exchange rate between (or price of) services and natural resources; it can be whatever they agree to. They could decide on a one-time price, a yearly fee, or a percentage of whatever is produced with the resource once privatized.

Gilligan and Mary Anne can decide that they have stronger or weaker rights to their holdings, but they can't assign full liberal ownership without denying equal access to resources to future people who might appear or to the future Gilligan and Mary Anne should they change their minds. The accord does not give Mary Anne true property, only Gilligan's agreement to refrain for now from using some resources that remain part of the nature reserve. But hopefully, this process gives an example that can be extended beyond the two-person case.

[2] In the two-person case, public spaces are not essential, but they quickly become essential in larger groups.

1.1 Equal Division or Compensation

The most obvious way to establish property by agreement is to divide it into equally valuable portions,[3] but the equal division is by no means the only possible solution or necessarily the best solution. Consider again the two-person example. Suppose Gilligan wants to hold all resources in common, and Mary Anne wants to divide them equally. There is no necessary reason one should have their way without the agreement of the other.

Within the environmental constraints, no fixed portion of available resources should necessarily be designated for division into private property, and there is more than one way to divide a thing. Suppose a ball drops from an airplane. They could divide it by cutting it in half across its equator or through any meridian, but they could just as well divide it in nonphysical ways, such as Gilligan takes every-other day, or they leave it in a designated place where either of them can use it when they want if they put it back when they're done. The same is true for fulfilling the requirement that both people try to stay out of each other's way as they both use natural resources to satisfy their needs and wants. Division and common ownership fulfill that requirement in different ways. Dividing some portion of resources and keeping another portion of resources in common fulfills that requirement as well. The question of what way is right depends on the wants and needs of both parties.

It is a mistake to think that we *must* divide resources into private parcels and that we can only create public parcels by contributing parts of our private share. This rule gives privatization a default position that it does not deserve. We could as well hold all property in common unless one individual can make an agreement with all other individuals to create a private sphere. I have dismissed the idea that there is any natural right to the property beyond what free people freely agree to. One might be tempted to conclude that, therefore, all property is held in common unless some agreement brings us out of that state, but this would be to assert that there is a natural right to common property. I have dismissed a natural right to property in any form. We have a claim to our status as free individuals with equal claim to use natural resources to meet our needs and wants, but we equally lack any specific claim to property in any specific form.

[3] George; Spencer, 141; Steiner, H. (1994). *An Essay on Rights*. Oxford: Blackwell.

There is no necessary reason why land must be privatized at all. People's need for privacy does not necessarily require fixed private property rights. Nomads can have privacy simply by a custom that keeps one group from pitching their tents too close to another group and that keeps everyone moving on after a certain period of time.

However, there are at least two reasons why some land must be held in common. First, if land is divided into more than four parcels with no public spaces at all, one person will find it impossible to interact with some of the others without gaining the permission to pass through a third person's property. Second, we will kill the ecosystem that sustains us if we alter too many resources.

If neither common ownership nor equal-size private holdings necessarily deserve default status, complications enter the question of what lost opportunities a person should be compensated for. Is a person entitled to an equal share of all resources or merely of all privatized resources? Suppose a large polity divides half its land into equal shares and holds the other half in common. Everyone has equal access to resources in that sense. Is Mrs. Howell entitled to compensation because she wants all of her portion in a private share and none in common assets? Or is the Professor entitled to compensation because he wants his entire portion as a share of common assets and none in private property? Arguments in later sections imply that both have some claim to compensation.

The argument for ECSO freedom in my earlier book should be thought of as a constraint on the distribution of property that provides one justification for a departure from equal shares.[4] Imagine an island populated by a giant and several dwarves. Imagine equal division provides each dwarf with enough to secure their physical needs and a substantial amount of luxuries, but it does not provide the giant enough to secure her vital needs. Without ECSO freedom the giant is effectively forced to be a servant of the dwarves to purchase access to the resources she needs simply to enjoy the same status freedom as everyone else. The implication is that everyone is entitled to a share at least large enough to maintain their status as a free individual if there are enough resources for all to have a share large enough to maintain that status. My earlier book discusses the

[4] Widerquist, *Independence*.

issue of what to do if there are not enough resources to secure everyone's ECSO freedom.[5]

There is some question about what equal division is. Is it equally valuable portions or portions that equalize welfare or opportunity for welfare? The previous paragraph argued for larger shares for people who need more to attain status freedom, but that argument does not necessarily imply equalization of welfare beyond that point. Return to the giant-and-dwarves example. Suppose that there are more than enough resources for everyone to maintain their status as free individuals and additional scarce resources available to put toward satisfying wants. The giant can argue that they should have a larger share so that they can attain the same level of welfare as the dwarves, and the dwarves can argue that they should all have equally valuable shares despite size differences. I have not put forward a theory that fully resolves this dispute. I am not sure it can be resolved.

Another problem with simple equal division is that it takes the size of the population as exogenously given. Under equal division, an individual is entitled to the total value of natural resources divided by the size of the population, whatever the population happens to be. The amount of resources a person can claim is subject to everyone else's fertility decisions (or the fertility decisions of the previous generation), and the amount of resources each person in the next generation can claim is subject to our fertility decisions. If the size of the population were to impose serious restrictions on core liberties, the moral claim could conceivably be the other way around, with each person's fertility options subject to maintaining a goal for the size of individual shares.

Both of those options are too restrictive. If human effort increases the value of resources, it might be possible to have a large population with sufficiently large shares available for everyone, but it might necessitate departing from equalizing the value of natural resources and/or external assets.[6] This issue could be important if an increase in output per person is accompanied by a decrease in resource availability and an increase in population.

Additionally, an equal division is not necessarily what everyone wants. Suppose Mr. and Mrs. Howell are more talented, diligent, hardworking,

[5] Ibid., 171–186.

[6] Ibid., 171–186.

and/or ambitious than the other castaways on Gilligan's Island. They want a larger share of property and a higher standard of living than everyone else, and they are willing to work for it in ways the others are not. It could be in the interest of all parties to grant the Howells a larger share of property, or even stronger rights of ownership than others, in exchange for their agreement to perform some sort of service for those who agree to make do with less property. One way to achieve this would be for everyone to own equal shares and the right to lease them out. Another way would be for those wanting larger shares and those willing to consider smaller shares to negotiate collectively, which might lead to a different outcome. There is no unique outcome or process. The agreed price could vary with the negotiation process and the incidents of ownership.

The above discussion implies that there is no one right price for external assets relative to services. There is no unique answer for the cash value of an equal share. There are only people's subjective evaluations of what an offer might be worth to them.

1.2 Full Collective Ownership

Conceivably, people could agree to a rule that all natural resources are strictly collectively owned. Although collective ownership with an individual veto over all resource use is unworkable and inconsistent with individual status freedom,[7] that decision-making rule is a very unpopular form of egalitarian ownership. Collective ownership tempered by a requirement of unconditional access to a sufficient amount of resources in the form of a UBI is possible. That rule would significantly limit collective power over individuals and resources, but it probably wouldn't be all that is necessary to counteract all potential dangers of excessively centralized control of resources, and I doubt most people today would want such pervasive collective ownership even if it were used as a commons.

[7] Cohen, 94–101; Widerquist, *Independence*.

1.3 Privatization by Accord

A property-rights accord is one way to create property rights for unowned resources. It is more flexible and avoids some of the problems with equal division and full collective ownership. It is simply the following: *one person establishes a property right in a natural resource by paying a negotiated price to everyone else for the duties their ownership imposes on them.* This agreement establishes "as-if property," an agreement to get everyone else to treat unowned resources as if they were property. Consider this process in an ideal form, in which everyone agrees.

Imagine a perfect market to create a property-rights accord using a Walrasian auctioneer,[8] a nearly omnipotent convener who calls out prices for all goods in a market. The auctioneer uses their powers to observe how much each potential market participant is willing to buy and sell at that price. If the quantity supplied and the quantity demanded of each type of commodity match, they allow trade. If not, they adjust prices in whatever direction seems likely to be closer to a match and announce again, repeating this process until there is a perfect match, and only then allow trade. If the auctioneer fails to find an equilibrium in which the supply of resources is equal to or greater than the demand,[9] resources remain unowned or common.

The only requirement for a property accord is some set of prices that could establish a set of property rights that everyone would willingly choose over leaving resources unowned and unownable. (Other fallback positions might be equally justifiable, such as equal division or unlimited access to the resources one can use oneself without the right to trade them, but I use unowned and unownable resources as the fallback position in my examples.) There might be many different Walrasian equilibriums that satisfy this requirement, and negotiating between them is an important problem, but the discussion here does not require that there be a unique solution.

[8] The unrealistic nature of the Walrasian auctioneer is not relevant to the problem at hand, because I'm not suggesting the market or any other institution can or do approximate it.

[9] Disequilibrium, in this case, is only a problem if demand exceeds supply. If there is no equilibrium, but if there is at least one vector of prices in which the supply exceeds demand, then it meets the qualification of establishing property rights by voluntary agreement.

The Walrasian auctioneer asks the following questions for each natural resource: at price x, for vector of rights y, in resource z:

1. How much are you willing to purchase for your own property?
2. How much are you willing to privatize to others in exchange for 1/nth share of the revenue?

By answering these questions, people determine how many goods are privatized, at what prices, and under what set of regulations.

The auctioneer asks these questions for every portion of each natural resource including land, minerals, water, clean air, and so on. People have to answer several other questions that don't necessarily have to be answered at the same time as the first two:

3. What would you prefer be done with the revenue from the privatization of resources?
4. Of the remaining resources, how much are you willing to make public property?
5. How much are you willing to leave unowned and in common?
6. How should collectively held resources be used and managed?

These questions are important, and they imply that the establishment and management of collectively held property is an important concern of a society committed to maximal equal freedom. Except for briefly touching on question 3 below, I set these questions aside, because this thesis focuses only on the establishment of private property, which is accomplished by the answers to questions 1 and 2: one person acquires the right to hold a piece of property by paying everyone else for the duties their ownership imposes on them and by following the rules the accord sets for privatization (i.e., by obeying regulations). This means simply that if you want to own an external asset, you have to *buy* it from everyone who has to make do with less so that you can have it. That is, from the rest of society. You cannot simply appropriate property or buy it from the previous owner or through the most common privatization method: have ownership assigned to you arbitrarily by the government because of your insider status.[10] You have to buy it from the people on whom you want to impose the duty to respect your right over that asset.

Once an agreement is reached, everybody pays a central authority for the resources they use, and this money goes to compensate everyone who has less. Under the unanimous agreement, the revenue could be used for anything at all. But without the unanimous agreement, there is a strong case for returning a large part of the money to people in cash so that they can use it for whatever they want. The government can divert funds for merit goods and other goals, but the goal of maximal equal freedom and of respecting ECSO freedom gives reason to use cash distribution as the default solution and to make sure that an individual has something of their own.

Assuming everyone would choose to own something, everyone would both pay into the authority and receive revenue from it. Assuming all funds are redistributed, those who hold more than an average-sized share pay in more than they receive back, and those who hold less receive back more than they pay in. Assuming some funds are devoted to public purposes, the average person will pay more in cash than they receive back in cash compensation. Net recipients can use their net revenue to buy services from others. The consumption of these services is their compensation for holding less property than everyone else. If no one wished to hold a disproportionately large share, and no revenue was required for public services, everyone would pay in exactly what they received back, and no money would need to change hands at all. But as long as people have different desires for property and different willingness and ability to trade services for them, some people will be net payers, and some will be net recipients.

This method of distribution has two similarities with Ronald Dworkin's clamshell auction—both have people bidding for resources and a Walrasian auctioneer,[11] but it is closer to Allan Gibbard's method, and perhaps even closer to the Gilligan's Island example summarized at the start of Chapter 2.[12] The method here is based on equally unowned resources, while Gibbard's is based on an equal share of ownership in

[10] Widerquist and McCall, *the Prehistory of Private Property.*

[11] Dworkin, *Sovereign Virtue*, 65–83.

[12] Gibbard. Dworkin does not cite Gibbard, and both neglect to cite Schwartz and Crawford.

resources. Gibbard spells out the solution in less detail and seems to fall back onto hypothetical rather than literal agreement.[13]

Dworkin's auction is designed to achieve an equal division of resources, while the JPA method is designed to achieve a mutually acceptable division that can deviate from resource equality. Thus, Dworkin uses a special currency (clamshells) that cannot be exchanged for anything but resources, while this method uses ordinary currency for resources. No one in Dworkin's auction is a net payer or a net recipient of the auction, although their bundles may be traded. To maintain resource equality over time, Dworkin creates a hypothetical insurance scheme to make sure that the distribution of resources is ambition-sensitive and endowment-insensitive.[14] Endowment-insensitivity is not a goal here. I assume people own their endowments and ambitions, and they are welcome to trade the benefits of those endowments for greater shares of external assets, as long as doing so is beneficial and agreeable to people with smaller shares of external assets. They are also welcome not to trade their endowments and to use them only to enjoy a minimum share of external assets.

This method is substantially different from and more consistent with maximal equal freedom than the prevailing system of full liberal ownership without consent or compensation to people who have less. Unlike that system, a first-best accord would create a form of property without imposing a noncontractual duty. Every liberty a person sacrifices to create a property for someone else is exchanged either for similar property or for services provided by property owners. Therefore, it creates no legal privileges; everything a rich person has is paid for and paid to the right people.

If a first-best accord were possible, it would promote each person's interest as they perceive it themselves. If the bargaining process is efficient, it exhausts all possible opportunities to improve people's welfare relative to their starting point, but efficiency is not an essential justification for it. If unanimous accord could be reached, it would not create equality, but it would create a form of property that is both more egalitarian and more consistent with maximal equal freedom than the full liberal ownership rights favored by right-libertarians and familiar in most countries today.

[13] Gibbard, 27–28.

[14] Dworkin, *Sovereign Virtue*, 73–83, 89.

Unfortunately, many barriers exist to achieving a property-rights accord in anything like a real-world example.

2 Three Barriers to a Property-Rights Accord

This section discusses three barriers to achieving a first-best property-rights accord: overlapping generations, the improbability of unanimity, and the desirability of revocability.

2.1 *Overlapping Generations*

This section points out problems with the institution of permanent ownership without a responsibility to compensate those on whom the obligation to respect property rights is imposed, but it should not be interpreted as suggesting any particular reform. Any solution will have to balance the property holder's need for stability against the nonowner's need to be free from excessive, uncompensated, and noncontractual obligations.

Although people in one generation might want to establish permanent, transmissible property rights, they cannot do so without interfering with the ways future generations might want to use resources and define property. Imagine a world in which humans mate like salmon at the very end of their lives. Suppose members of each generation are born and die together with no overlap between lives at all. Wilt Chamberlain and other great basketball players live in this society. They play and negotiate so well that all of their contemporaries sign over the use rights to all natural resources now and forever. But of course, they're going to die of old age just as the next generation is born. How are they going to bring the next generation into this agreement? They could leave a note for subsequent generations explaining the "agreement" signing over rights to all external assets to the heirs of basketball players. When the next generation is born and reads the note, they can reasonably object that it's not really an "agreement:" no one asked them whether they agreed or not; nothing binds them to follow it. It is not a voluntary agreement on their part. It amounts to nothing but attempted external interference.

The above discussion implies the need for something stronger than an inheritance tax. Even if basketball players lived twice as long as everyone else, if they provided services only for the earlier generation, any special claims the earlier generation might have given them over external assets are noncontractual obligations imposed on the next generation without agreement from them or compensation for them. When the next generation is born, they are propertyless because of an agreement that was not voluntary on their part and is not binding on them.

How well must Chamberlain play for generation A to earn the power to decide which member(s) of generation B control access to natural resources and the external assets we make out of them? Infinitely. If we're concerned with maximal equal freedom, there is nothing one generation can do to justify imposing uncompensated noncontractual duties on members of future generations. This observation exposes a flaw in most existing property systems, which take the agreement of existing holders as sufficient reason for an individual to obtain permanent control of a resource and thereby obtain the privilege of interfering with the next generation of people who never agreed to privatize that resource.

Of course, people in one generation often create things that directly benefit subsequent generations. Imagine Shakespeare writes great plays in one generation that last for all generations to come. If Shakespeare, his descendants, or his trading partners (e.g., his publisher) carry over exclusive rights to his plays to subsequent generations, they have a greater claim on property than other members of the next generation, but they have obtained this greater claim without the agreement of those generations. If Shakespeare could travel in time and make an agreement with future generations saying that he will only write these plays if they respect his copyright in their generation, he might be able to make a genuine agreement. But he cannot travel in time. He can only make agreements with his contemporaries, and so he must decide whether the amount he can make from his contemporaries is enough to make it worthwhile for him to write his plays. If the rewards are not enough, he does not write plays, or he keeps his writing secret. If the rewards are sufficient, he writes the plays, accepting that they eventually become public domain.

Other people do things that benefit future generations by altering physical property rather than creating purely intellectual property. Suppose Michelangelo alters blocks of marble in ways everybody likes. His contemporaries are willing to give him much larger shares of use rights to goods in his time in exchange for this service. But if they also confer permanent ownership of Michelangelo's sculptures to him or to people in the next generation he designates, they interfere with subsequent generations in the same way that a permanent copyright would interfere with future, would-be readers of Shakespeare. It is interesting that current law gives Michelangelo and his successors' permanent rights to his creation but not Shakespeare, when the whole value of Shakespeare's work is his intellectual creation while a portion of Michelangelo's work is a natural resource to which his claim is no more "natural" than anyone else's.

This discussion implies that no generation can establish permanent property rights, which in turn implies both that the discussion of the assignment of property rights must be ongoing (see below), and that the discussion applies not only to natural resources but to all external assets or at least all assets produced by earlier generations. That is, time limits that are applied to copyrights can be extended to physical improvements to natural resources. People can negotiate voluntary rewards in the form of services from their contemporaries, but any rewards they claim from future generations are not voluntary. This argument applies not only to Shakespeare and Michelangelo but also to Locke's original appropriator and to the value of any improvements made to the resource value of ordinary goods by past generations. Thus, the property in question is extended from natural resources to external assets (or at least those external assets altered by previous generations), implying limits to property rights discussed below.

2.2 *The Improbability of Unanimity*

A lack of agreement is not necessarily a failure of the Walrasian process; it might simply mean that no price makes it worthwhile to establish property rights rather than remain in the default position in which external assets remain unowned. If property rights make far greater production possible, at least one deal is probably better for everyone, but even then, reaching it by unanimity is unlikely. One problem is that the unanimity rule is not necessarily optimal or free from manipulation.[15] Another problem is that, in an ongoing negotiation of property rights, it is not possible to return to the default position. If a large number wants an agreement that a smaller number finds objectionable, they can't simply go back to nonownership as people did in the two-person example.

Suppose one person or a small group holds out and refuses any price (or every price that anyone else can afford) for accepting the property

[15] Mueller, D. C. (1989). *Public Choice II*. New York: Cambridge University Press, 43–53, 96–111.

rights of others. Some might genuinely prefer some other social arrangement to the one on offer; others might have unrealistic beliefs about how much they can get. If society imposes one kind of property-rights regime on a small group of people who prefer something else, it interferes with that group's freedom to use resources the way they want. But if the small group forces the large group to remain in the state in which resources remain unowned, the small group interferes with the larger group. It is not certain which of these two actions constitutes greater interference, and there is no natural default position.

One partial solution to the problem of a lone holdout is that all equally situated individuals receive and pay the same amount regardless of their bargaining stance. That is, if A, B, C, and D have the same characteristics and the same share of the property, D can hold out until the four of them get a better deal, but D cannot hold out until D gets a better deal than A, B, and C. Even with this rule, it is likely that some net recipients will reject something that is acceptable to the majority of net recipients. It is not necessarily morally impermissible to hold out in the designated default position in hopes of achieving the best deal possible. That sort of action is the basis of voluntary exchange; the two sides of the transaction do without the benefits of exchange unless or until they come to an agreement. But without a natural default possibility, the agreement won't be completely voluntary, and the approximation of a property-rights accord runs the risk that it will either give too much power to dissenters or force them to accept burdens unwillingly. The section on non-ideal theory discusses how to balance these concerns.

2.3 *The Desirability of Revocability*

It is likely that many people will not want to make an irrevocable agreement to create property rights, but will want the power to revise that agreement if it turns out to be less desirable than expected. It is problematic for society to place individuals in a position in which they *must* choose between a permanent, irrevocable agreement and no agreement at all and far worse to resort to the after-the-fact rationalization that disadvantaged people would have agreed if there had been an agreement.

Also, even if people are initially willing to make an irrevocable agreement (such as marriage without the possibility of divorce), there are agreements that people ought to be able to revoke, and irrevocability causes problems when people change their mind whether or not they initially agreed to sign an irrevocable contract. Revocability would not be a problem if binding agreement were all there was to social justice, but from the standpoint of the greatest freedom, it is not certain that the freedom of the person who wants to maintain a binding agreement always trumps the freedom of people to get out of a bad agreement.

For these reasons, I stress justice as "accord" rather than "agreement" or "contract," a truly just society is one in which everyone truly agrees at any given moment, not one in which somebody signed—or, more likely, hypothetically signed—some binding agreement in the past no matter how much they now wish they hadn't. The goal here is to approximate accord rather than convince ourselves that we have a hypothetical agreement and that all those who don't agree are behaving unreasonably or violating rights.

The need for revocability has to be balanced against the desire for a secure agreement. The more permanent the agreement is, the greater the problem of people who are stuck with an agreement they want to revoke, but the less permanent the agreement is, the greater the problem of insecurity of expectation. Again, there is no ideal solution. The non-ideal solution will involve balancing competing concerns such as these.

3 The Approximation of a Property-Rights Accord in Non-ideal Theory

If a unanimous agreement is not possible, it is important to remember that maximal equal freedom for all is not complete freedom for all. The goal is to minimize rather than to eliminate interference caused by whatever rules are created. However, a simple majority rule, giving the majority power to impose whatever it wants on the minority, is not enough. The widest possible agreement with the minimum impact on dissenters achieves the maximal freedom consistent with equal freedom for all.

Although it is beyond the scope of this thesis to specify the exact institutional setting for determining a property-rights regime, I suggest five limits to the property rights that follow from the above discussion. First, from the discussion in my earlier book, the government must not alienate anyone's status freedom (ECSO)—or aid anyone's self-alienation.[16] Second, the protection of ECSO freedom ensures the consent of net payers but not net recipients. Third, there cannot be a dichotomy between a one-time assignment of property rights and subsequent trade. Fourth, any agreement must seek to minimize its impact on people who do not wish to be a party to the agreement. Fifth, legal authority also has a responsibility to protect buyers' access to the property.

3.1 *Inalienability of ECSO Freedom*

My earlier book argued that the government has a strong responsibility to refuse to enforce any contract alienating an individual's status as a free person.[17] According to Arthur Kuflik, authors such as Kant, Locke, Rousseau, and Spinoza concur for various reasons and to various extents.[18] John Stuart Mill and John Gray have made similar arguments.[19] Those who oppose inalienability do so on the basis of some right of contract[20] or something like a right to wave rights.[21] My earlier book argued that such theories justifying so-called voluntary slavery effectively put the promotion of positive opportunities ahead of government's primary responsibility to protect the individual's core liberties from interference. ECSO freedom is a core liberty. The right to sign any contract one might be offered is not. Therefore, the government has a responsibility to refuse to enforce any contract alienating a person's status freedom.[22]

My earlier book carries this reasoning further to protect the level of functioning necessary to maintain ECSO freedom. Along with chattel slavery and involuntary servitude, people may not sell themselves into such severe economic destitution that they are effectively forced to

[16] Widerquist, *Independence*.

[17] Ibid., 57–59.

[18] Kuflik, A. (1984). "The Inalienability of Autonomy." *Philosophy and Public Affairs* 13, 271–298.

[19] Mill, J.S. (1965). *The Essential Works of John Stuart Mill*. New York: Bantam Books, 348; Gray, J. (1983). *Mill on Liberty: A Defense*. London: Routledge & Kegan Paul, 93.

[20] Nozick, 331.

[21] Steiner, *An Essay on Rights*, 64–65, 71–72, 232–233.

[22] Widerquist, *Independence*, 57–59.

work for others.[23] This responsibility implies a substantial constraint on the property-rights agreement: the government cannot enforce any agreement that allows people to become economically destitute. Therefore, certain kinds of agreements cannot be irrevocable, and agreements alienating ECSO freedom cannot be enforced at all.

Modern contract law rightly refuses to enforce contracts that explicitly alienate an individual's status as a free person. Currently, the failure to fulfill a contract cannot be grounds for imprisonment,[24] corporal punishment, or any other denial of an individual's status freedom—except impoverishment. If we recognize propertylessness as a threat to freedom, as my earlier book argued, the same kind of prohibitions against selling oneself into slavery should also apply to protecting people from severe economic deprivation. The government must refuse to assist in self-alienation of ECSO freedom by refusing to honor any contract alienating an individual's claim to the property they need to maintain their free status, and by refusing to impose propertylessness on anyone.

This argument does not imply that the defendants should pay no financial penalty at all for breaching an agreement, but they may declare bankruptcy while keeping enough property to secure their ECSO freedom. This justification for a social minimum could be called by a name that might sound oxymoronic—permanent, starting-gate sufficiency. It allows each person the right to return to an acceptable starting point that secures their ECSO freedom. It is equivalent to bankruptcy without destitution. Permanent, starting-gate sufficiency implies that no one can be deprived of their status as a free person by contract or trade or other people's trades, but severe violations of criminal or civil law such as negligence, accidental bodily harm, and paternity might be grounds on which a person's ECSO freedom could be alienated. Governments have abused the powers of imprisonment, but I do not explore the issue of exactly when the government can and cannot deny a person's status freedom.

This argument has implications for the treatment of UBI. Assuming that UBI is in place and set just at the level that secures a person's basic needs, it could not be used as collateral for a loan and would be a protected asset in the event of bankruptcy (with the exceptions above noted). However, if the UBI is set higher than that level, a portion of it

[23] Ibid.

[24] Except in the case of criminal negligence.

could be used as security for a loan and could be seized in the event of bankruptcy.

More important than the government's responsibility to refuse to enforce agreements alienating ECSO freedom is its responsibility not to impose (or force an individual to accept) the loss of ECSO freedom. As long as it is possible to create some property-rights regime that protects everyone's ECSO freedom, the government may not impose a property-rights regime that denies it to someone. If no possible property-rights regime protects everyone's ECSO freedom, the government must limit everyone's ECSO freedom in the same way and to the same extent.[25]

3.2 ECSO Freedom Assures the Consent of Property Holders

The protection of ECSO freedom has a centrally important role for the rest of the property theory laid out in this chapter. It establishes the maximum amount the government can interfere with an individual's access to external assets. At most, it may limit a person's access to resources to just enough to secure their basic needs but not more than that. So, the person who has the minimum access to resources is also subject to the maximum amount of interference of any citizen who hasn't been convicted of a crime. If a person wants more than the minimal amount of external assets, they have to buy them not only from the last generations' holders but also from the government as representative of the people. People who want more than a minimum amount of external assets have rights similar to buyers in private transactions.

Any person who chooses to buy a greater amount of property has, in that sense, voluntarily accepted the conditions. If I buy a car for $40,000, I might think the price was too high but I could have kept my money, or I could have chosen to work less instead of earning the money to buy the car. This is how the term "voluntary trade" is normally used. It does not mean that I like the price, or I think the price was fair, but it means that I *accept* the price, when I could have said no. This condition makes all of the net payers in this property-rights regime voluntary taxpayers. If they want to live with a modest amount of property, ensuring a life that is not thoroughly bad in an absolute sense,[26] they may do so, and no one will

[25] Widerquist, *Independence*, 171–186.

[26] Ibid., 32.

force them to do anything else. If they are more materially ambitious than that, and they wish to hold a greater share of resources, they may choose to accept the terms and conditions of holding a greater share of resources. Participation in the economy needs to be voluntary to that extent, and if it is, it establishes the voluntary agreement for everyone who lives above the minimum.

We normally consider the portion of the cost of going to the previous owner as the "price" and the portion going to the government as a "tax," but both parts of the purchase price of a good, represent two interested parties: the person who previously held the special right to that external asset and the people who are burden by the obligation to respect that external asset and the resources that went into it have been privatized. Taxation, therefore, does not interfere with established property rights or with self-ownership rights. People choose to pay taxes in the same way and for the same reasons that they choose to pay the private cost of goods. They might complain that either or both prices are too high, but they accept them willingly as free persons.

This method does not, however, establish the voluntary agreement for those who live at or near the minimum. They hold less property than everyone else, and they receive compensation for that fact in the form of money with which they may purchase services provided by everyone else, but their acceptance of this compensation does not indicate that they have willingly accepted others' greater shares because they have no other option.

3.3 No Dichotomy Between Initial Assignment of Property Rights and Subsequent Trade

The problems of overlapping generations, dissent, and revocability all imply that there cannot be a dichotomy between an initial allocation of property rights and subsequent trade of property. No group of people at any one time in history can confirm full, permanent ownership rights over an external asset in the sense of all of Honoré's eleven incidents.[27] To do so would be to attempt to make a contract binding on generations of people who were not signatories to it. The process of maintaining a coalition in favor of the property-rights system must be continuous, and that

[27] Honoré.

process must be balanced against property owners' need for stability, and most importantly, everyone's desire to make long-term plans and to know what their rights are when they agree to use, rent, access, or purchase resources, whether they are owned publicly or privately.

One way to create such a balance would be to define all property as fixed-term leases, which have to be renegotiated at expiration. Each person at any time could buy a lease for a one-time fee or a regular rent for a period of say 20, 50, or 100 years or the lifetime of the buyer. It is in no one's interest that all property rights terminate after one week or one year. The government could retain the right to regulate property, which is some of the right to manage the property (incident 3), and it may or may not sell the right to trade and transfer the titles it has created (incidents 4 and 5). However, if these are temporary leases and no matter how many times a piece has been transferred, the lease still terminates at its expiration date. Potential purchasers might not want to buy temporary leases. Many people understandably desire the feeling of permanence, but mortal beings do not need infinite open-ended property rights to have that feeling. The solution involves balancing. The fixed-term-lease solution might be cumbersome and difficult to administer, and its distributional goals might be achieved much more simply through the tax system.

Although the government could create property in almost any combination of Honoré's eleven incidents[28] (with the exceptions noted), it need not make radical changes to achieve the necessary goal. It could simply keep the familiar institution of full liberal ownership of property with only one change: the liability to execution (incident 10) could be explicitly extended to include the responsibility to pay a tax sufficient to maintain the widest possible property-rights agreement and/or to minimize interference with dissenters from the agreement. The tax rate would have to be variable to avoid imposing the regime on future generations, but it should not vary widely in a short time, because owners need some secure expectations to make long-term plans.

One simple solution is a wealth tax and/or rent and resource value tax redistributed as a UBI. Either of these taxes or their combination is essentially a rental price for holding external assets.[29] I have elsewhere

[28] Ibid.

[29] A natural resource tax could be used instead; an income tax or a combination of taxes are also possible. The argument here does not imply that it must be a wealth tax,

discussed the value of land-value, rent, and resource taxes.[30] Here I focus on a tax on all wealth, although I see it as a complement to rather than a substitute for land-value, rent, and resource taxes.

Each year, people pay a percentage of their wealth into the UBI fund. Potential owners are warned that all property is subject to that tax and that the government may raise or lower that tax as needed, and they may revise their present decisions to purchase property based on the knowledge that policy might change again in the future. The government's ability to change the tax rate has to be balanced against wealth holders' need for security. Therefore, the government must not lead people to believe that taxes will remain low and suddenly raise them to confiscatory levels as soon as owners have improved the property in some way. Perhaps changes in the tax rate should be announced well in advance and phased in over a period of years.

If wealth holders do not want to pay an announced increase in the wealth tax, they can divest themselves of their wealth and live off the UBI. In the same way: if my landlord announces that my rent will go up next year, I can decide to pay or I can move out of his building.

If the wealth tax is not excessively high or variable, it leaves the private property-rights system basically in place and raises enough revenue to end propertylessness and to justify property rights on a contractual basis. If a revisable wealth tax is in place, there is no need for time-limited property rights, confiscatory inheritance or income taxes, or any major disruption of basic market exchange to make the agreement in the interest of people with less property now and in subsequent generations.

3.4 *Minimizing the Negative Impact on Those Who Are Not Party to the Agreement*

Because no property system without unanimous agreement eliminates interference, and unanimous agreement is nearly always impossible, the

and the choice of which type of tax to use depends as much on empirical efficiency concerns. The argument does imply that there should be specific kinds of natural resource taxes, such as taxes for depleting nonrenewable resources or fines and fees for polluters, but these specific issues are beyond the scope of this thesis.

[30] Widerquist, "A Permanent Endowment for the United States"; Widerquist, "The People's Endowment"; and Howard and Widerquist, "Why Link Basic Income to Resource Taxation?".

best possible system attains the widest possible agreement and minimizes its impact on the people outside the agreement. There might be a conflict between the goals of achieving the widest agreement and minimizing the negative impact on dissenters.

If people cannot agree on one property system, the first solution to seek is a way to divide resources so that everyone has a proportionate amount of resources to devote to their uses, and diverse lifestyles are possible. Earmarking resources for various uses is not always practical, but if compensation is paid in cash, the cash can be used to buy resources, finished goods, or services to put toward the kind of lifestyle individuals prefer. To minimize the impact of an agreement on people left outside, society should be careful not to set compensation payments too low or give them in a form that people might not want.

The requirement to minimize the negative impact on dissenters implies the need for a UBI in cash and for the highest sustainable UBI. Arguably, the property-rights regime that sustains the highest (cash) UBI creates the most realistic options for those who do not want to be a part of the agreement. Therefore, it has the minimum negative interference with dissenters. Suppose a plurality wants a market economy with reasonably strong private property rights, but other groups want other things (e.g., a hunter-gatherer economy or a socialist cooperative society); separation is not possible, and there are not enough resources for each group to introduce their system as fully as they'd like. Any group (even a majority) that imposes their system on others interferes with them to some extent. If the majority merely imposes their system on everyone else without compensation, they substantially and significantly interfere with everyone else's attempt to lead their lives in their own way. If they make resources available to dissenting minorities, giving them some ability to lead their chosen lifestyle, they do not eliminate interference, but they reduce its significance. If one of the many possible kinds of market economy can give dissenters a higher UBI than all other systems, that system interferes least with dissenters.

If all net recipients were willing participants, they could choose to accept compensation in the form of specific services or public goods. But if there are unwilling people who are being compensated, a cash component becomes extremely important, because money can buy any resource and any finished product. Therefore, arguably, cash compensation gives dissenters the widest opportunities to use compensation to pursue their chosen lifestyle. Otherwise, there is the possibility that people would be forced to accept less of everything and who are given "compensation" in the form of something they do not want. Imagine the government privatizes the resources you could use to sustain your life and compensates you with free, subsidized Greco-Roman wrestling. If you don't like Greco-Roman wrestling, the public center would provide no compensation at all.

However, there are limits to what cash compensation can do, and the concept of the "highest sustainable UBI" is notional. If there were a fixed amount of privatized resources under a fixed set of regulations, the highest sustainable tax on those resources redistributed as a UBI would provide the "highest sustainable" level. But none of these things are fixed. The government could probably increase revenue by renting out all government-owned land—including all local, state, and national parks and the entire road system—and eliminating all regulations on privatized resources. But those policies are not likely to minimize negative interference with dissenters. And so, when someone uses the phrase, "highest sustainable UBI," it should be understood as maximizing revenue for a given set of regulated, privatized resources. However, strategies for publicly held property and public services should also be thought of both in terms of maximizing the benefit to all and minimizing the negative impact on dissenters.

3.5 *Protection of Property Owners*

The above discussion rules out permanent, full ownership rights without compensatory taxation for the (otherwise) propertyless, but it leaves the people free to define property in a wide range of ways. Property could be anything from fixed-term leases to permanent ownership subject to adjustable tax rates and regulations. In other words, property does not naturally entail transmissibility, the absence of term, and residuary character,[31] but these incidents can be bought by the liability to taxation (strong version of incident 10) if the price is agreeable to both parties.

The social agreement to create property needs to retain some of the right to manage (incident 3) and the right to income (incident 4). For example, society could privatize the land along a river subject to the restriction that owners maintain a footpath along the river, do nothing

[31] Honoré's incidents 7, 8, and 11, see above.

to pollute the river or disturb traffic on the river and make no loud noises that would disturb others in the area. The rights of the private holder here are similar to the rights of a potential renter of property. I might want to rent a house with the right to tear out the walls, repaint it, and remodel it, but I cannot force the owner of the house to rent it to me under those conditions, and I might not be able to afford to buy those rights. Remember, the goal is to give people (including future generations) the biggest equal opportunity to use the resources of the Earth to satisfy their needs and wants. To do so, you need not only to make sure everybody gets something but also to regulate some of the uses that have negative effects on others.

However, potential buyers in this market should have more rights than renters have in the private market. Restrictions on property rights have to be balanced against the potential owners' equal freedom to use resources to satisfy their needs and wants, which requires both security and equal access to external assets.

Laws regulating property should not be used to make any particular lifestyle impossible unless it uses more resources or creates more negative externalities than potential buyers are willing to pay for. If some kinds of resource use pose a danger to others, they might have to prohibit it outright. For example, society can prohibit outright an activity that releases plutonium into the atmosphere because it creates a cost that the polluter cannot possibly pay for. It can prohibit an activity that releases a harmless substance into the atmosphere that will turn the sky orange, simply because the person who wants to do this cannot pay others enough to make them willingly accept an orange sky. But if someone wants to live a loud lifestyle, society should try to find an area where people can be loud without disturbing others.

Like cases must be treated alike. Society can charge more for uses of property that take up more resources or have more harmful activities. It cannot charge more for people who want to use resources to build a temple to Isis than it charges for people who want to use the same amount of resources to build a temple to Zeus, simply because the majority wants to promote the worship of Zeus. If a person or a group of people do not demand a disproportionate amount of external assets (or are willing to pay the required compensation) and are not posing a danger to others, they must not be prohibited from the assets they need to practice their lifestyle in a society that provides the maximal equal freedom.

These protections for property buyers and holders are strong enough to ensure that extensive markets cannot be prohibited.

There is, of course, a Coase Theorem problem in determining what constitutes harm,[32] especially in *advance* of the assignment and definition of property rights. This is an involved legislative issue, but I will suggest two guides. First, the default is to leave the environment alone. People who want to change the sky from its natural blue to an artificial orange have more to prove than those who want to leave it as we found it. Second, people who get their way compensate those who do not. Part of an individual's UBI compensates them for the fact that they cannot turn the sky orange or release plutonium into the atmosphere, which they could do if they were either alone or in a world of like-minded people. Wealthy people might be disgruntled that they aren't even wealthier, but have gotten their way with more people: they are net contributors to the BIG system because they control, use, or use up more of the Earth's resources than nonwealthy people. If they think the services they provide for the rest of humanity are worth more than they are receiving, they are welcome to stop participating and live off the UBI.

4 A Left-Libertarian Reply?

A left-libertarian might reply that the concerns with property rights expressed in these chapters are contained in left-libertarian theories of justice and they can be solved by left-libertarian policy prescriptions. This section argues that the concerns I have expressed are broader than the concerns of better-known, left-libertarian theories and that while left-libertarianism prescribes a unique solution, the negotiated solution proposed here could have many different, but equally legitimate, outcomes.

According to Peter Vallentyne's definition, "Left-libertarian theories of justice hold that agents are full self-owners and that natural resources are owned in some egalitarian manner."[33] By that definition, JPA property theory is arguably left-libertarian. Although JPA does not assume

[32] Coase, R. H. (1960). "The Problem of Social Cost." *Journal of Law and Economics* 3, 1–44.

[33] Vallentyne, P. (2000). "Introduction: Left-Libertarianism—A Primer." In *Left-Libertarianism and Its Critics: The Contemporary Debate*, Peter Vallentyne and Hillel Steiner (ed.). Basingstoke: Palgrave, 1–20, 1.

external assets are naturally collectively owned, it assumes that resources are equally unowned by everyone and that society is committed to maximal equal freedom. The subtle difference in these assumptions leads to only subtly different outcomes. I could list a lot of points of agreement. For example, most left-libertarians agree that the equal right to use external assets is consistent with maximal equal freedom for all and that unequal ownership of natural resources without compensation is inconsistent with equal freedom. But this section discusses several ways in which JPA property theory differs from the better-known forms of left-libertarianism.

Left-libertarianism is most often associated with the idea that natural resources are the only legitimate tax base: the government should tax away all of the resource value of assets, but it should not tax labor or improvements made to natural resources.[34] Therefore, many left-libertarians would reject the arguments above that extended the tax base from natural resources to all external assets and extended the possible forms of taxation from eco-taxes to income and wealth taxes. Some left-libertarians might argue that the lack of a dichotomy between resource taxes and wealth or income taxes implies a rejection of full self-ownership, but I argue that is not the case.

Rather than rejecting self-ownership, JPA theory rejects the belief that income or wealth taxes infringe on self-ownership. These taxes infringe on property ownership, not self-ownership. The income aspects of self-ownership entail a right to negotiate with others for property. If society as a whole has a legitimate claim to all external assets, it is a party to any transaction, and therefore, it can tax any transaction involving external assets or claims on external assets. The rights to mix one's labor with an asset, increase the asset's value, and resell the asset for a higher price are incidents of ownership of *the asset* that the holder must buy from others. If I live in a rental house, and I alter the rental house, increasing its value by 100-fold and then resell it, the owner ought to be able to sue me to have his entire house back, not only the value before I improved it. If I want to own the rights to alter it and sell those alterations for profit, I must negotiate this with the owner of the house. We might agree that I will receive 99% of the value of my alterations or only 1% of the value of my alterations. We might not come to any agreement at all, and I might

[34] Spencer; George; Vallentyne; Steiner, *An Essay on Rights*, 235–236.

have to choose not to rent or buy the house. If I am capable of increasing the value of the property and the owner is wise, they will give me a good incentive to do so, but it's their house, their decision. We both have to decide whether to accept or reject the terms of trade. There is no fixed or objective "value" of labor or natural resources. There are only subjective valuations and negotiated prices.

Most left-libertarians do not focus on the need for social agreement. Most of them view resource taxation as an application of the Lockean proviso on unilaterally appropriated resources rather than the rejection of unilateral appropriation altogether. Therefore, most left-libertarians (1) do not argue that the incidents of ownership are subject to social agreement, (2) take the quantity of privately held natural resources to be approximately fixed, and (3) believe legitimate tax revenue is determined by the market value of natural resources (variously defined). If 1 and 2 become subject to agreement, 3 is no longer fixed. Applying observation by John Christman more broadly,[35] there is no unique solution to the question of how to value human effort relative to natural resources, only the opportunity to negotiate.

Without a need for social agreement, the policy implications of left-libertarianism are relatively clear, if not unique, as can be shown in the following graph. The horizontal axis shows the percentage of resources held privately. Point 0 on the left corresponds to a society with no private ownership of property and Point 100 on the right is the point at which all external assets are private property. The vertical axis shows the price of holding resources privately. The downward-sloping line labeled with the large D is a demand curve relating the price of holding resources privately to the quantity of resources private citizens are willing to hold. Under normal assumptions, the demand curve generally slopes down from left to right, showing that the lower the price, the more people are willing to buy.[36]

[35] Christman, John (1994). *The Myth of Property: Toward an Egalitarian Theory of Ownership*. New York: Oxford University Press.

[36] People are not always willing to buy more at lower prices, but that assumption is not essential for the process here.

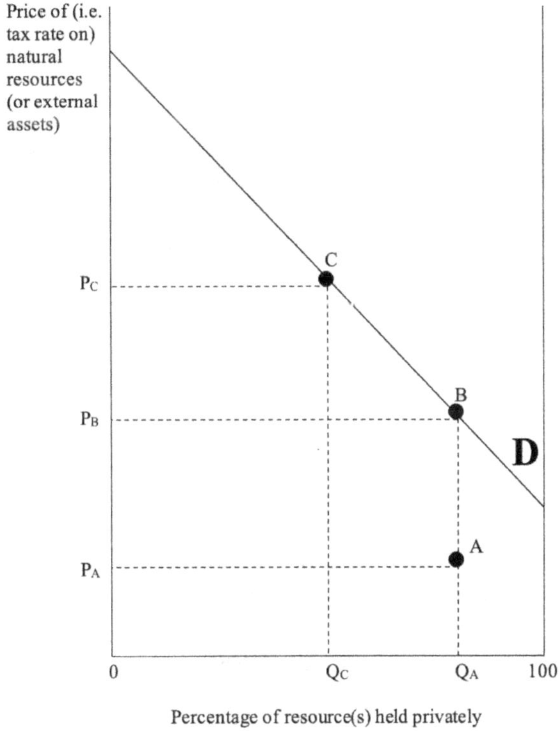

The left-libertarian complaint is that the price for holding natural resources privately (the resource tax) is less than the market price. Graphically, current property law puts society at a point like A inside the demand curve on the graph. Property owners hold Q_A and pay only P_A for it in taxes, although a competitive market or an auction would force them to pay P_B. Point A would not necessarily violate equality of access to natural resources, if holdings of resources were rationed so that everyone had an equal amount. But, of course, resources are not rationed. Some people have more access to them than others. People who control resources resell them to the rest of society and realize gains equal to the difference between the market price and the actual resource tax multiplied by the quantity.[37] These excess gains are attributable to the scarcity value of natural resources rather than to some valuable service provided by the

[37] $Q_A (P_B - P_A)$ to express it mathematically.

people who own them. If society charged P_B (reaching point B on the demand curve) and used the proceeds to fund public projects, a welfare state, or a UBI, it would achieve equal access to resources and freedom as noninterference more fully than right-libertarianism.

If Q_A is taken as given, left-libertarianism implies that achieving point B is the unique solution to the problem of private property. A tax rate of P_B fully satisfies the requirements of left-libertarian justice as usually understood. In the introduction to the principal anthology on left-libertarianism, Vallentyne writes, "For natural resources, there is a fixed supply, so we can here focus solely on how the competitive value is determined by demand."[38] Supply, the willingness to designate natural resources as private property, and negotiation of the price of privatization play no role, and the empirical question of the competitive value of natural resources becomes extremely important. However, although the amount of natural resources in the world is approximately fixed, the amount of natural resources in private hands could be highly variable and subject to discretionary government regulations and other policies that affect value. This fact gives the social agreement enormous price-setting power, which is usually ignored by left-libertarians. Estimates for the value of natural resources currently in private hands vary enormously. Optimistic estimates give great leeway for redistribution and leave little leeway, but much left-libertarian literature hinges on that empirical question.

My criticism of left-libertarianism is that the legitimate tax is not determined by the empirical question of the market value of natural resources. If the actual market value of natural resources (or the relevant external assets) is close to the higher figure, the left-libertarian solution is sufficient. However, an argument for redistribution sufficient to free people from abject poverty does not hinge on that fact, because the *price* of privatizing natural resources is a key subject for social agreement. If government policy achieved point B, but P_B was not sufficient to make people with lesser shares accept the agreement to establish property, maximal equal freedom for all would not be realized. P_B *might* be sufficient to establish an accord, but if not, there is room to negotiate a higher price, which might involve moving to a point like C (or any point along the demand curve) at which the price of (tax on) resources is higher, fewer resources are held privately (more being unowned, used collectively,

[38] Vallentyne, 16.

or kept in reserve for future generations), more regulations are placed on the use of privatized resources, and the share of income attributed to human resources is lower. Q_A is merely the percentage of resources that are currently in private hands. It is not certain that the portion of resources currently held privately is optimal. The arguments above imply that the government should use its price-setting power to obtain the widest possible social agreement in favor of the property-rights regime and to minimize interference with those who dissent from the agreement.

In other words, the solution is more complex than the equalization of the current market value of privately held natural resources, but there are several reasons why the question is more complex still. First, it is not simply a matter of choosing what percentage of all external assets to privatize, but the percentage of each asset to privatize. A social agreement might result in privatizing 90% of society's copper, 50% of its zinc, 20% of its oil, 1% of its ancient artifacts, and 0% of its plutonium. Flexibility in the quantity of each resource to privatize implies flexibility in the price of each resource. The social agreement might choose to use much more of its price-setting power for some resources than others. Second, as argued above, there are different rules under which external assets can be privatized. The incidents that potential owners are bidding for will affect the price they are willing to pay, and therefore the outcome is very far from being tied to the current market price of natural resources or external assets.

If ECSO freedom is a constraint on the process, the government should (if necessary) use its price-setting power to ensure that everyone has at least enough income to secure their basic needs. Although taxes directly on resource value have many advantages, taxes that are only indirectly connected to resources (such as income, sales, and wealth taxes) do not need to be excluded from policymakers' toolkits. All of them are taxes not on humans or human labor but on the acquisition of external assets, and all external assets are made at least partly out of natural resources. Thus, JPA is different from much left-libertarian theory, such as that of Van Parijs and Steiner, who argue that the just amount of distribution is a purely empirical question that has nothing to do with whether it provides enough to live on.[39]

[39] Van Parijs, *Real Freedom*; Steiner, *An Essay on Rights*.

5 A Right-Libertarian Reply?

This property theory provides an answer to Nozick's question about "redistributive" taxation:

> Why should we treat the man whose happiness requires certain material goods or services differently from the man whose preferences and desires make such goods unnecessary for his happiness? Why should the man who prefers seeing a movie (and who has to earn money for a ticket) be open to the required call to aid the needy, while the person who prefers looking at a sunset (and hence need earn no extra money) is not?[40]

The man who wants to earn extra money works for the tax authority for the same reason that he works for the employer, client, or landlord: he wants a larger share of external assets, and these are the people who can reward him with it. If he does not want to own a relatively large share of external assets, he need not work for his employer and he need not be a net taxpayer. If he wants to own a relatively large share of external assets, he must pay for them through "redistributive" taxation. If he wants to hold a large share of property without paying that tax, he simply wants something for nothing. He wants to take more resources and the things we make out of them without doing anything for those who must, therefore, make do with less.

One cannot use the theory presented in this chapter to justify any kind of tax, such as an arbitrary tax or a confiscatory tax designed to make certain lifestyles impossible. Anyone concerned with freedom is correct to argue against such taxation. But this theory counters the assertion that taxation in general is freedom-inhibiting. Quite the reverse: unequal ownership of property without redistributive taxation is freedom-inhibiting.

6 Conclusion

This chapter has argued that a justification for property consistent with maximal equal freedom for all requires property rights to be established by an agreement between those who assume rights of property and those who thereby have duties imposed on them. I've described the idea only

[40] Nozick, 170.

in the broadest terms. I have a lot more to work out. The contract must be mutually beneficial in the sense that those who assume larger shares of property must compensate those who accept smaller shares sufficiently to make property in both parties' interest. This objective can be achieved by subjecting property to a wealth tax or resource tax redistributed as a UBI.

In a modern economy or a right-libertarian ideal state, people who claim ownership say, "This is mine, because I have paid for it," but they know they paid only the person who held it before them, connecting through a long line of exchanges to a person who was arbitrarily granted ownership by some past government and that by holding that claim, other people to have been forced to accept less access to resources without their consent or compensation. The holder might have worked hard for their property, but they paid the wrong people. Property rights by approximate accord, as proposed here, allows a person to claim ownership, saying, "This is mine, because I paid the right people for it. Everyone, who has less directly benefits from the services I provide: I have paid compensation to everyone who must make do with less access to resources because I control the resources embodied in this asset; I have received the consent and followed the regulations of the majority." It is the holder's property because they paid the right people. They have a far stronger ethical claim to ownership than under any theory of unilateral appropriation.

Note: This chapter is a brief and preliminary statement of JPA property theory. I discuss other aspects of it in "A Permanent Endowment for the United States," "Why Link Basic Income to Resource Taxation?," and "The People's Endowment."[41] And I hope to develop it more in the future.

[41] Widerquist, "A Permanent Endowment"; Howard and Widerquist, "Why Link"; and Widerquist, "The People's Endowment."

CHAPTER 7

Conclusion: The Greater of Two Goods

I often quote myself. It adds spice to my conversation.

—George Bernard Shaw

A UBI-supported, voluntary-participation economy is not Utopia, but it would be a fundamental change in the goals or activities of the economy. It does not make the economy fully fair or completely just, but it does something for you. It protects you from abject poverty and propertylessness. Once a sufficiently large UBI (and a good housing policy) are in, no one in your society is unable to afford a home. No one must search for food in other people's garbage cans. No one is forced to accept the terms and goals of participation dictated by the people who control external assets. A few people refuse to participate at all. Some of them use UBI to start alternative communities; others use it to get their lives together. But most people do participate. They accept the arbitrariness and the unfairness inherent to the economy, but they accept it as free people, not as subjects who are effectively born into servitude. Many people still work long hours, but they do so because they have chosen this as a way to get ahead, not because they must accept it to survive. Most people agree that the benefits they get from economic participation make

K. Widerquist, *The Problem of Property*, Exploring the Basic Income Guarantee, https://doi.org/10.1007/978-3-031-21948-1_7

it worthwhile for them to accept its inherent casino element.[1] Some will continue to dissent, the economy described above provides more freedom and flexibility to dissenters than any other feasible system.

1 Freedom as the Motivation for Protection from Propertylessness

Any meaningful theory of freedom needs to have a theory of which freedoms are most important to protect. My earlier book (based on Part One of my thesis)[2] argued that the most important freedom to protect is a person's status as a free individual, which I define as effective control self-ownership (ECSO freedom): the effective power to make or refuse voluntary agreements with other individuals. It argued that capitalism with full liberal ownership of property does not protect ECSO freedom, because propertylessness makes a person effectively unfree. It also argued that many egalitarian theories that incorporate contributive obligations also fail to protect ECSO freedom. A person has ECSO freedom if they are not forced directly or indirectly by any means, including the economic necessity to serve a boss, a partner, or a social project. If people lack ECSO freedom because laws dividing up the Earth have made them propertyless, their freedom has been taken away by the law. A healthy adult can preserve their own ECSO freedom with access to a sufficient amount of raw resources or an in-cash UBI. The preservation of ECSO freedom does not necessarily entitle a person to cash. However, I have argued that a sufficiently large, in-cash UBI might be the most feasible and efficient way to preserve ECSO freedom in a modern industrial economy.

This book (based on Part Two of my thesis) focuses on the relationship between property and freedom in the more familiar liberal notion of "negative freedom" or "noninterference." This notion usually assumes that freedom is "scalar:" "a continuous variable" that can be measured by degrees on a scale. It rejected Lockean and right-libertarian theories of unilateral appropriation as failing to justify property consistently with the maximal equal freedom for all. From the assumption that natural resources are unowned, it argued that there is nothing an individual can do unilaterally to make them owned but that an approximation of

[1] Widerquist, *Independence*, 9–17.

[2] Ibid.

legitimate property rights can be created by the approximation of an accord. People attain a piece of property by paying others so that it is in their interest to treat that unowned resource as if it was their property. If property is held unequally, this provides an argument for a wealth-tax-financed UBI, in which anyone with a relatively small share is a net recipient, and anyone with a relatively large share is a net payer. Because it is compensation-based, this argument provides a reason for UBI in cash. Compensation is nearly always paid in cash to give the recipient the greatest discretion over how to use it. Conceivably, people could receive the cash compensation on top of the raw resources they received to secure their ECSO freedom, but doing so would allow people to buy their way out of the work needed to turn the raw resources into the goods they want. It might prove simpler and easier to provide the entire amount in cash.

2 How Big?

The two main parts of my 2006 thesis (the first part published as *Independence, Propertylessness, and Basic Income* and the second part published as this book) each argued for a UBI at least large enough to do a certain task. The earlier book argues for a UBI at least large enough to secure ECSO freedom. Chapters 2–6 of this book argue for a UBI large enough to approximate the property-rights accord—which is likely to entail the highest sustainable UBI. Putting the two pieces together implies that the actual level should be the greater of the two. If ECSO freedom were an overriding priority, UBI would have to be at that level, even if it were unsustainable. But of course, it makes no sense to set UBI at a higher than sustainable level except in the extraordinary circumstance in which the population is dropping more quickly than the sustainability is running out. In such a case, although the current level is unsustainable given the current population, we are taking action that will make it sustainable quickly enough for us to treat that level as sustainable. Barring that occurrence, it might be tempting to fall back on the empirical argument that, given the amount of industrial activities devoted to providing for things other than needs, the possibility that the minimum level of UBI needed to secure ECSO freedom is unsustainable is very unlikely. My earlier book argued that if a UBI high enough to secure ECSO freedom were to prove unsustainable, the UBI should be set at the level needed to secure ECSO freedom for the highest sustainable number of years of each person's life and that the rest of the time should be a period of national service that is equally demanding for all people regardless of social or individual advantage.[3]

3 Equality of Freedom

These two books were written from a standpoint of concern for both freedom and equality. Equality of resources, equality of welfare, or equality of standard of living have not played a strong part, but equality of freedom has, and the concern for the greatest equal freedom has led to a concern with a degree of equality of resources and standard of living. The concern is first to secure the most important freedoms for each individual, and beyond that to secure the maximal equal freedom from interference for every individual—including the interference caused by the initial assignments and maintenance of private property rights in natural resources.

The concern with freedom and property rights provides a message for both left and right.

If you are not on the side of the least advantaged, you are on the wrong side. If you're not for making the least advantaged as free from authority as you possibly can, you are not really on their side.

If you are not on the side of freedom, you are on the wrong side. If you're not for the freedom of the least advantaged from all authority (including the authority of the people who own stuff), you are not really on their side, and therefore, you are not really on the side of freedom.

[3] Widerquist, *Independence*, 171–186.

Index

K. Widerquist, *The Problem of Property*, Exploring the Basic Income Guarantee, https://doi.org/10.1007/978-3-031-21948-1

L

M

N

CPSIA information can be obtained
at www.ICGtesting.com
Printed in the USA
LVHW080954170223
739747LV00002B/19

9 783031 219474